Georges Seurat:
111 Colour Plates

By Maria Tsaneva

First Edition

*****

<u>**Georges Seurat: 111 Colour Plates**</u>
*****

Foreword

An important Post-Impressionist French painter, Georges Seurat moved away from the apparent spontaneity and rapidity of Impressionism and developed a structured, more monumental art to depict modern urban life. For several of his large compositions, Seurat painted many small studies. He is chiefly remembered as the pioneer of the Neo-Impressionist technique commonly known as Divisionism, or Pointillism, an approach associated with a softly flickering surface of small dots or strokes of colour. His innovations derived from new quasi-scientific theories about colour and expression, yet the graceful beauty of his work is explained by the influence of very different sources. Initially, he believed that great modern art would show contemporary life in ways similar to classical art, except that it would use technologically informed techniques. Later he grew more interested in Gothic art and popular posters, and the influences of these on his work make it some of the first modern art to make use of such unconventional sources for expression. His success quickly propelled him to the forefront of the Parisian avant-garde. His triumph was short-lived, as after barely a decade of mature work he died at the age of only 31. But his innovations would be highly influential, shaping the work of artists as diverse as Vincent van Gogh and the Italian Futurists, while pictures like A Sunday Afternoon on the Island of La Grand Jatte have since become widely popular icons.

Georges Seurat first studied art with Justin Lequien, a sculptor then attended the Ecole des Beaux-Arts in 1878 and 1879. After a year of service at Brest Military Academy, he returned to Paris in 1880. He shared a small studio on the Left Bank with two student friends before moving to a studio of his own. For the next two years he worked at mastering the art of black-and-white drawing. He spent 1883 on his first major painting, a huge canvas titled Bathers at Asnieres.

After his painting was rejected by the Paris Salon, Seurat turned away from such establishments, instead allying with the independent artists of Paris. In 1884 he and other artists (including Maximilien Luce) formed the Societe des Artistes Independants. There he met and befriended fellow artist Paul Signac. Seurat shared his new ideas about Pointillism with Signac, who subsequently painted in the same idiom. In the summer of 1884, Seurat began work on his masterpiece, A Sunday Afternoon on the Island of La Grande Jatte, which took him two years to complete.

Seurat studied avant-garde painting techniques, especially Impressionism and the latest scientific theories pertaining to light and colour. From 1885 to 1886 he developed the divisionist depicting. This new style, which consisted of systematically applied small touches of unmodulated colour, was based on contemporary optical theories of colour relationships.

Two years after his first Neo-Impressionist work was shown at the Salon des Independants, Seurat exhibited A Sunday on La Grande Jatte at the eighth and final Impressionist group show in 1886. His disciplined technique exerted a considerable influence over Neo-Impressionist artists such as Camille Pissarro, Henri Edmond Cross, and Paul Signac.

Seurat died in Paris on 29 March 1891 at the age of 31. The cause of his death is uncertain. His last ambitious work, The Circus, was left unfinished at the time of his death.

Paintings and Drawings

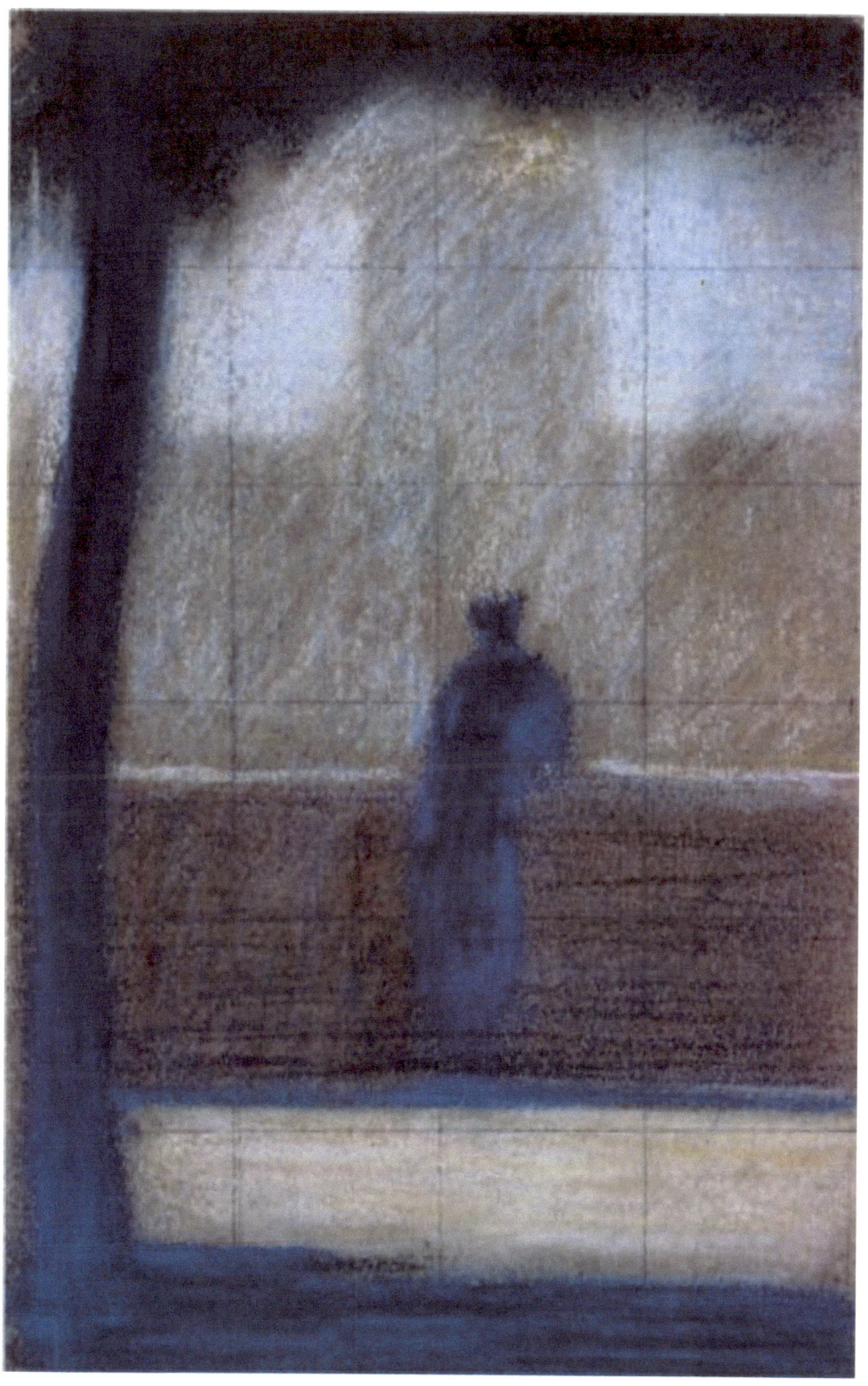

Man leaning on a parapet, 1879, pastel

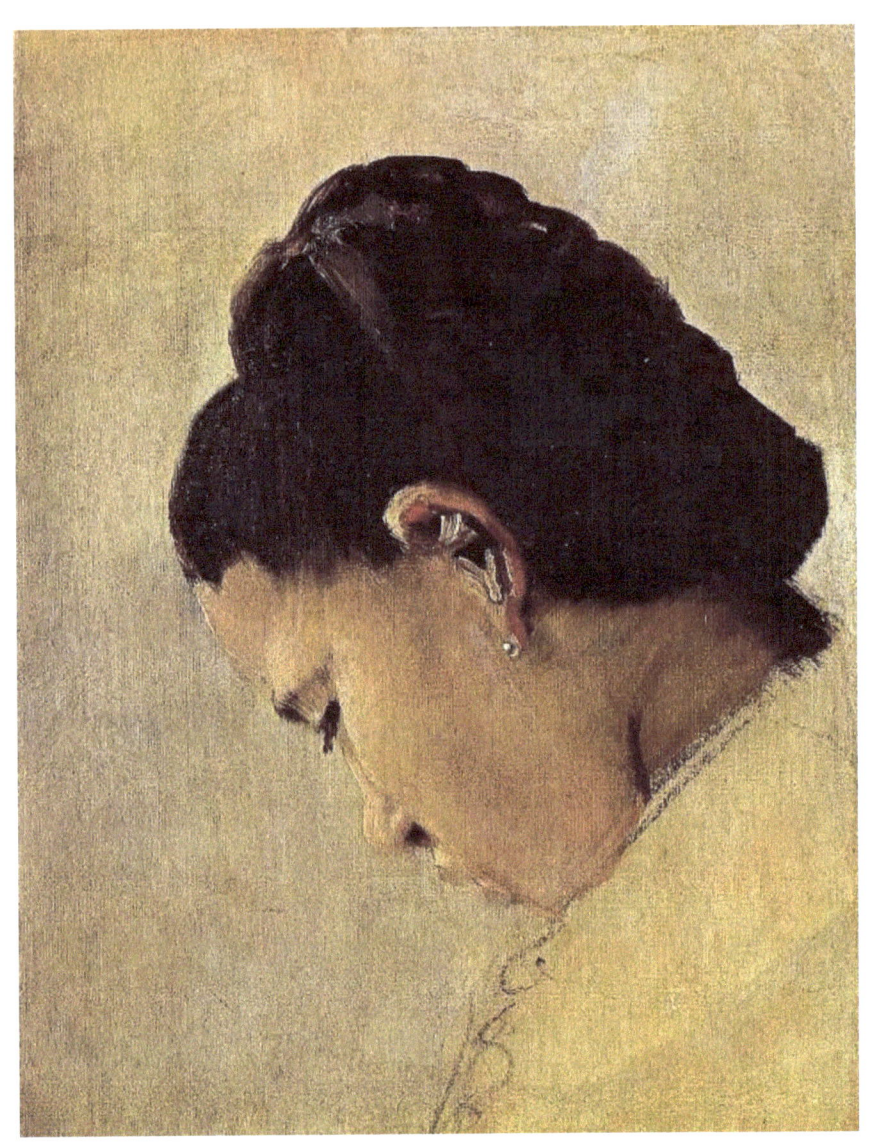

Head of a Girl, 1879, oil on canvas

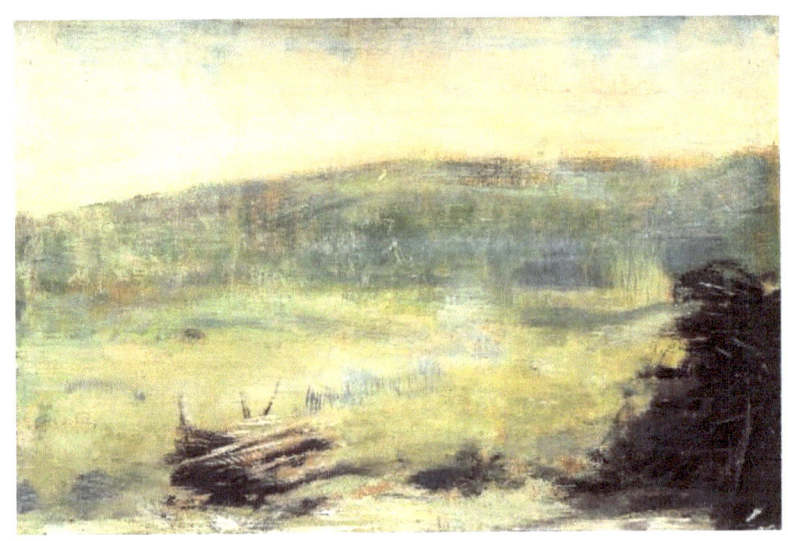

Landscape at Saint-Ouen, 1878-1879, oil on wood

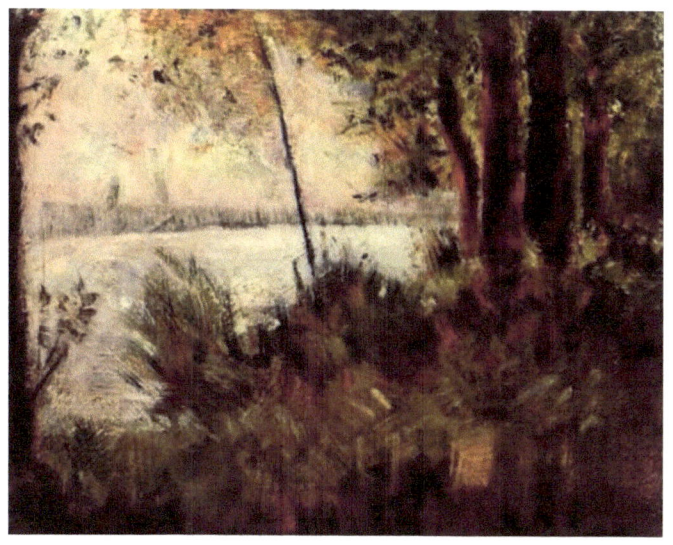

Grassy Riverbank, 1881, oil on canvas

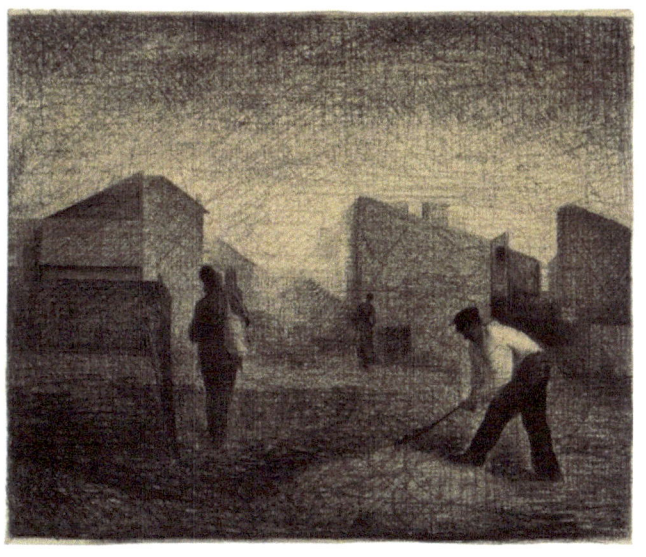

Stone breakers, Le-Raincy, 1881, crayon

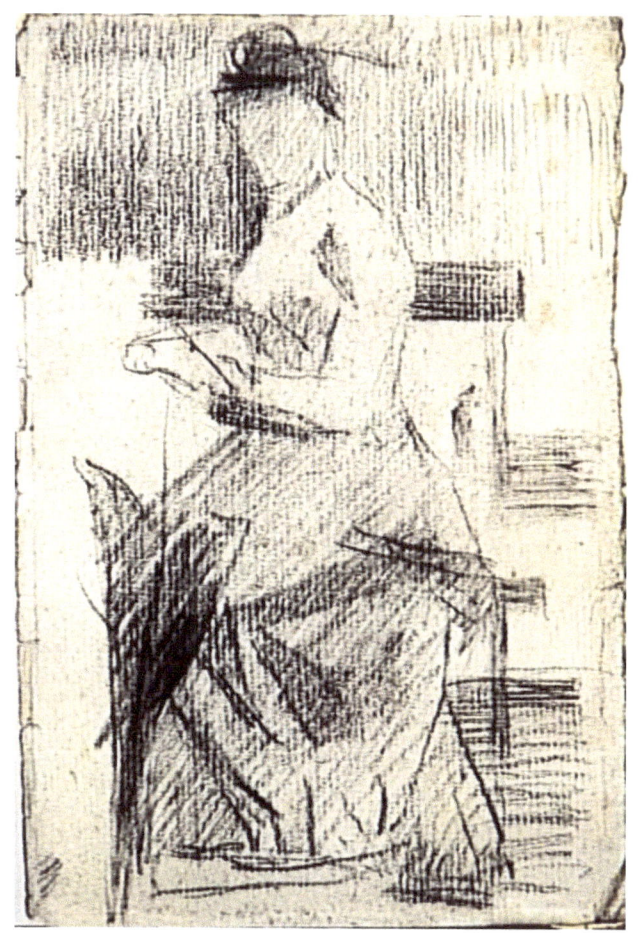

Seated Woman, 1881, crayon

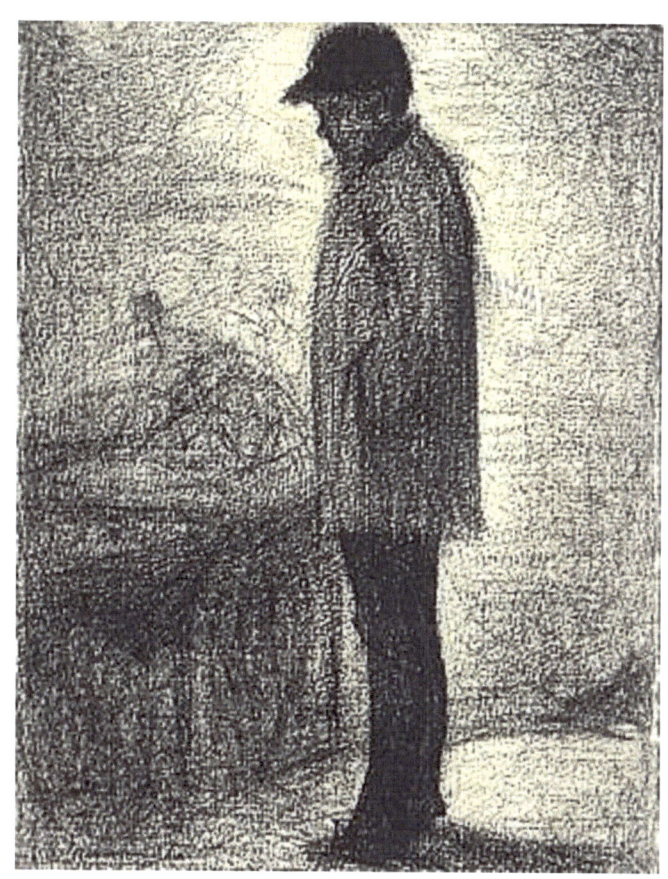

The seller of oranges, 1881, crayon

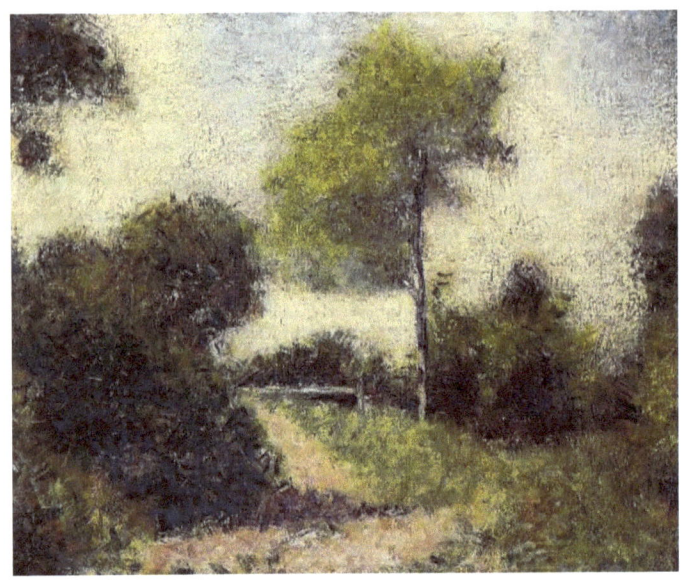

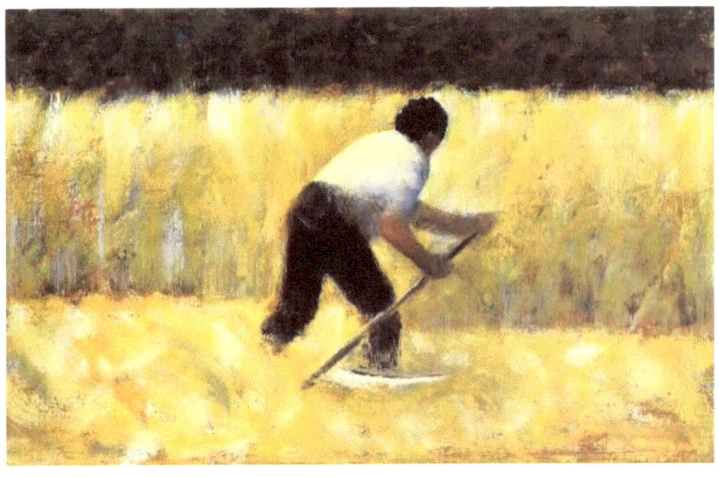

The Mower, 1881-1882, oil on wood

The Hedge (also known as The Clearing), 1882, oil on canvas

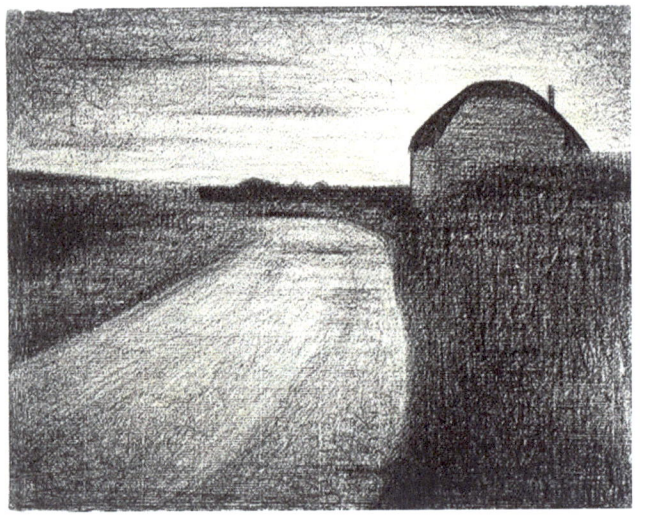

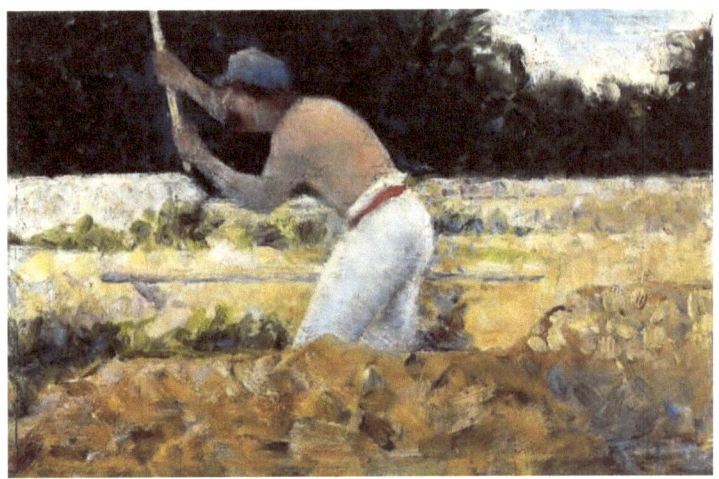

The Stone Breaker, 1882, oil on wood

On the road, 1882, crayon

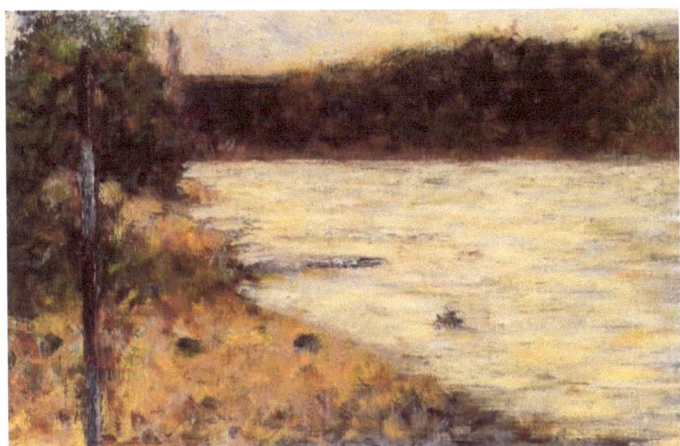

A River Bank (The Seine at Asnieres), 1883,
oil on wood

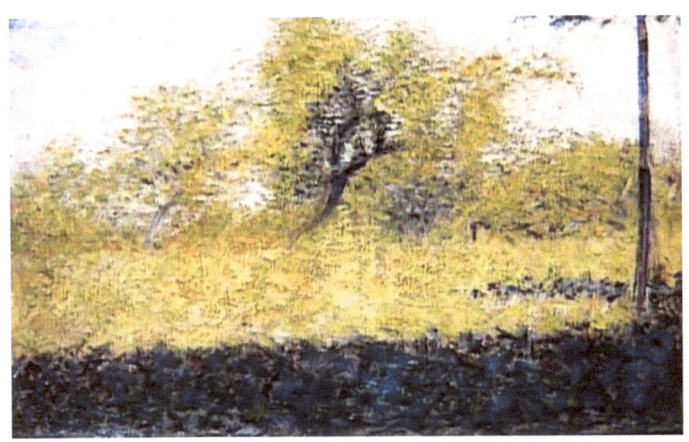

Edge of Wood, Springtime, 1883, oil on
wood

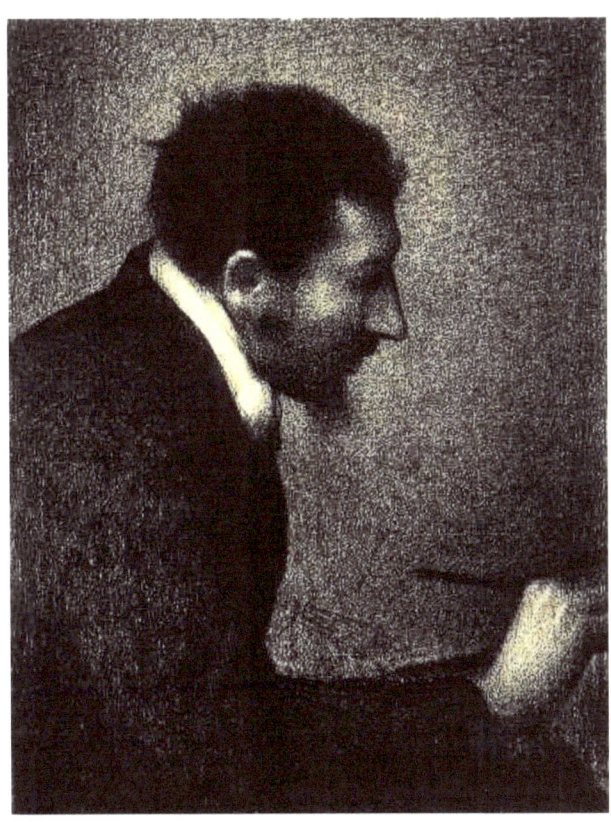

Portrait of Edmond-François Aman-Jean,
1883, crayon

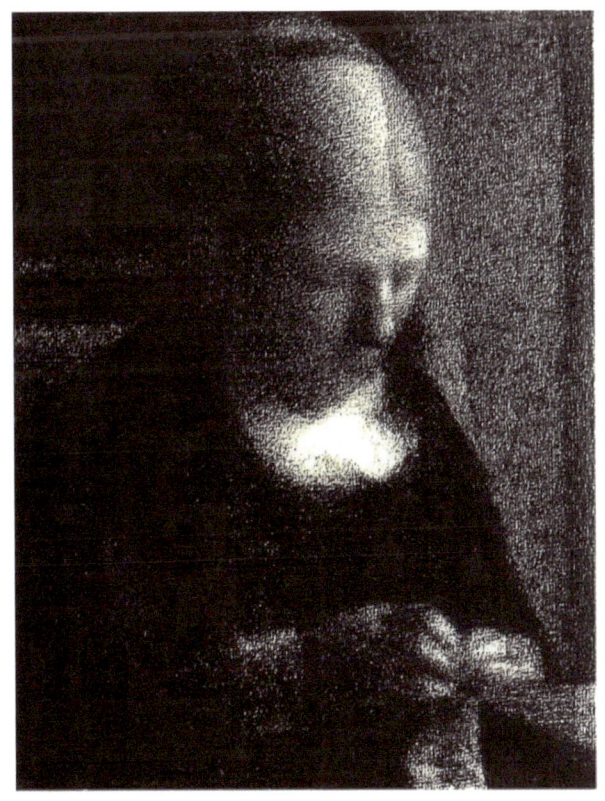

The Artist's Mother, 1883, crayon

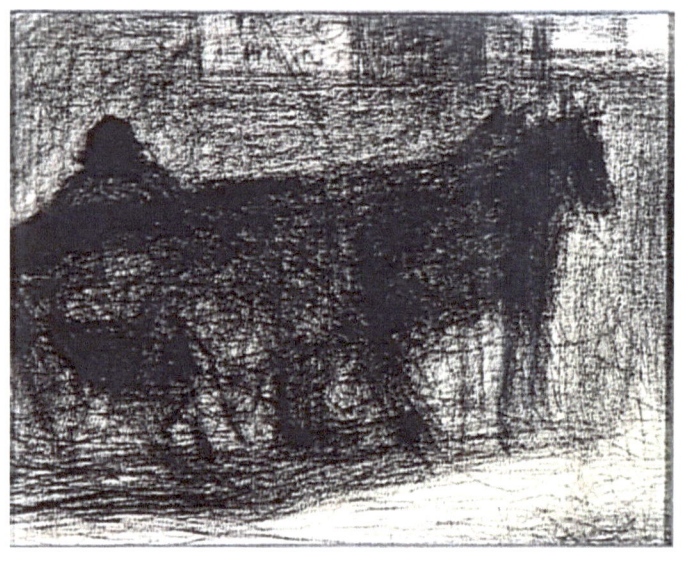

Two-horse hitch, 1883, crayon

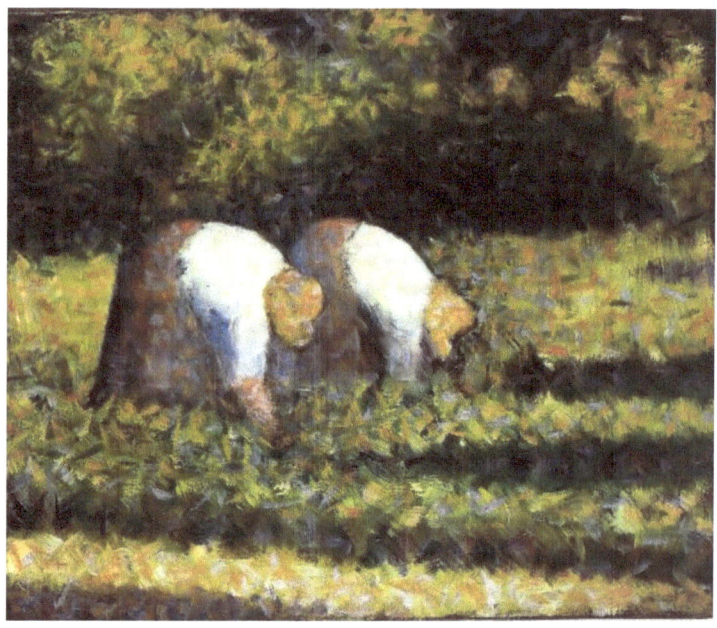

Farm Women at Work, 1882-1883, oil on canvas

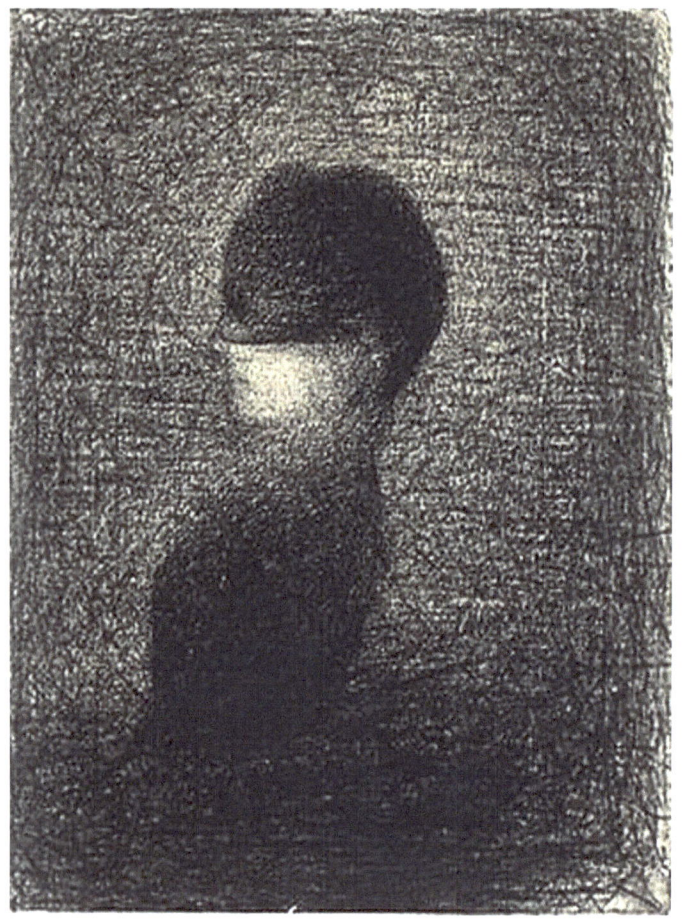

Voilette, 1883, crayon

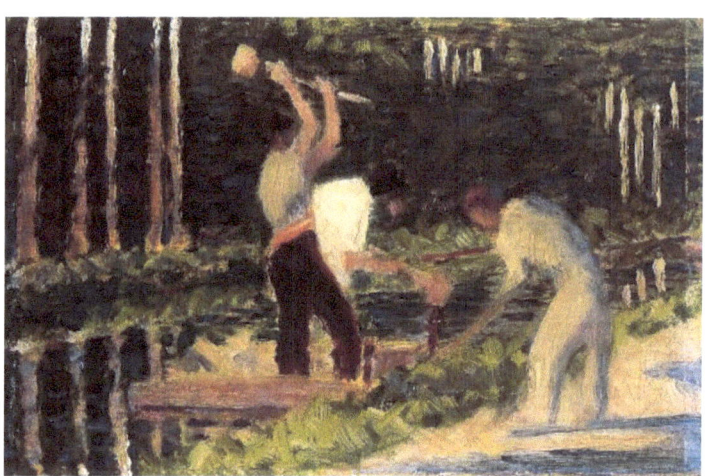

Men Laying Stakes, 1882-1883, oil on wood

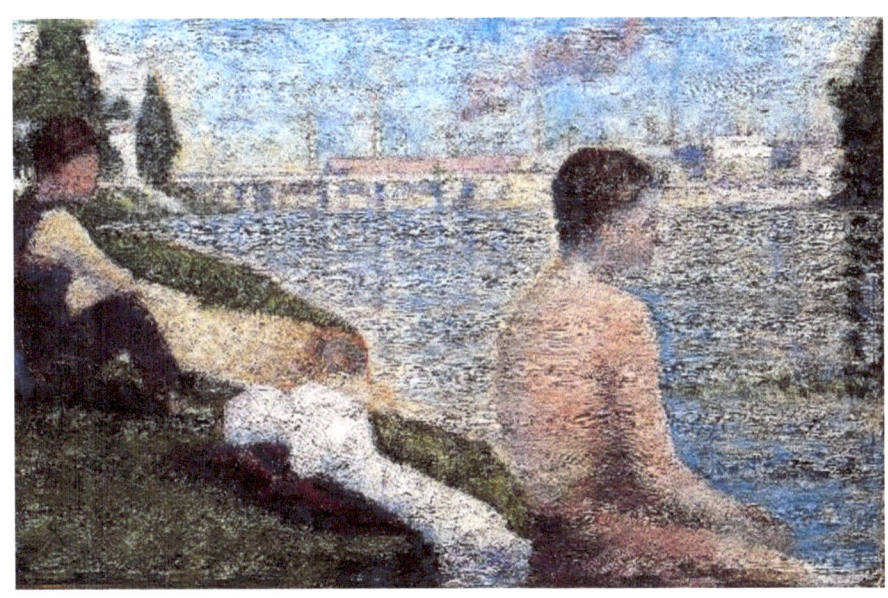

Seated Bather, 1883, oil on wood

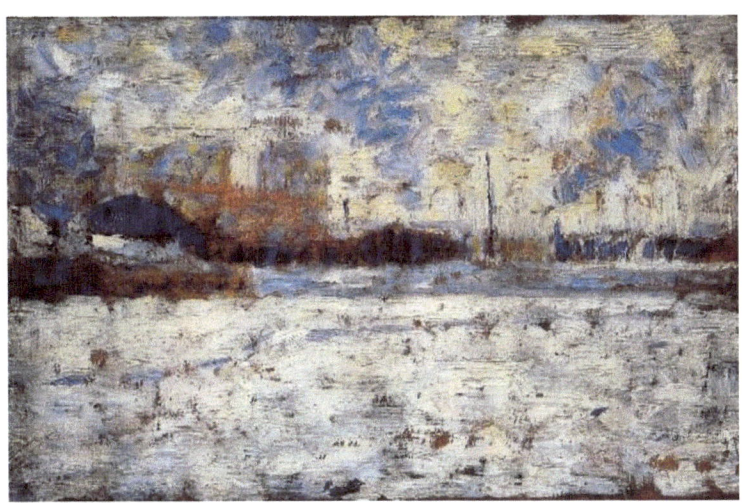

Snow Effect: Winter in the Suburbs, 1882-1883, oil on wood

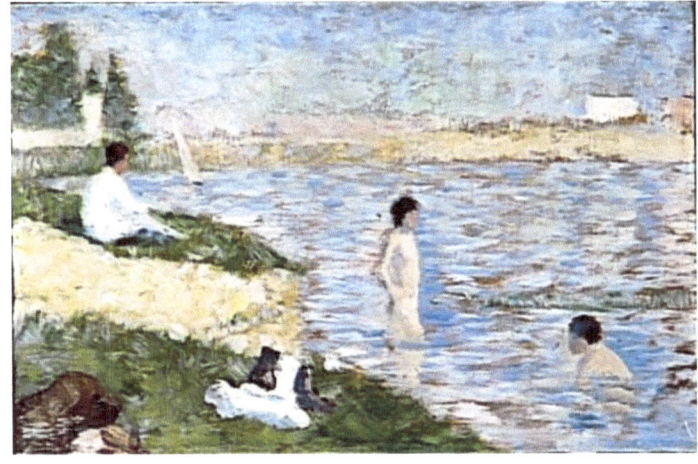

Study for "Bathers at Asnieres", 1883, oil on wood

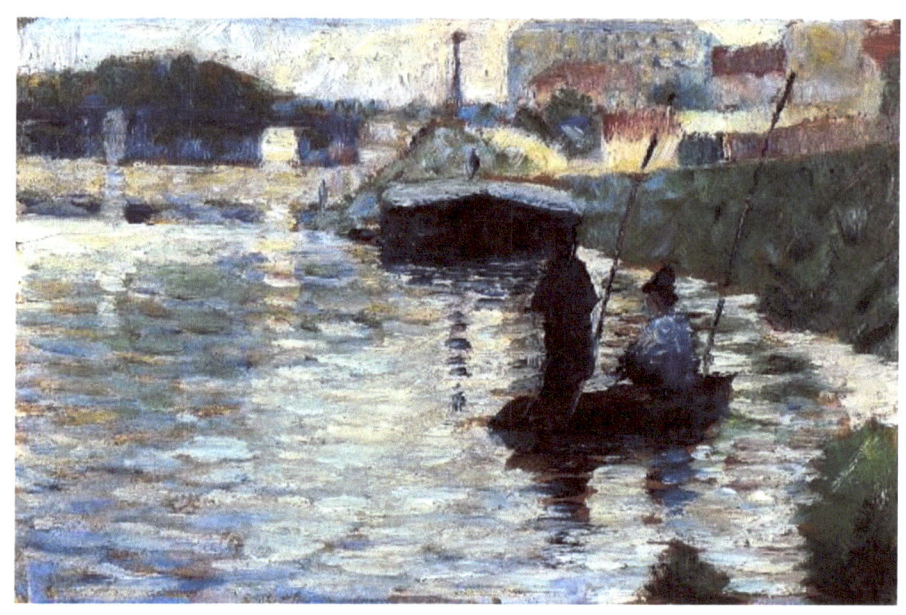

The Bridge - View of the Seine, 1882-1883, oil on wood

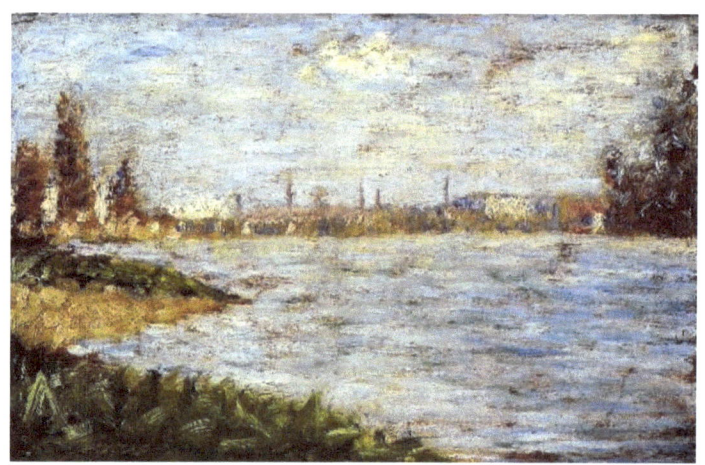

The Riverbanks, 1882-1883, oil on wood

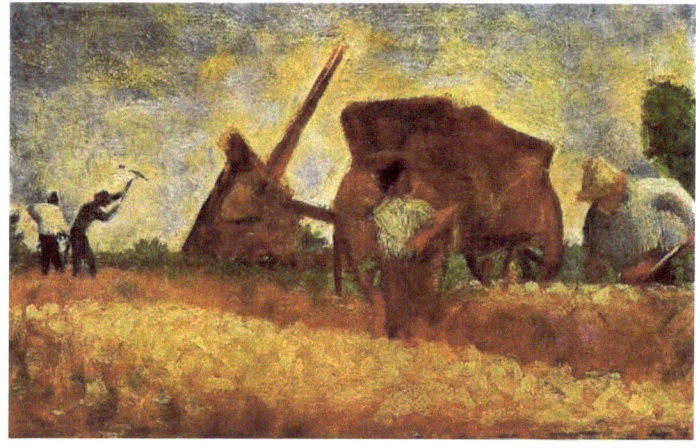

The Stone Breakers, 1883, oil on wood

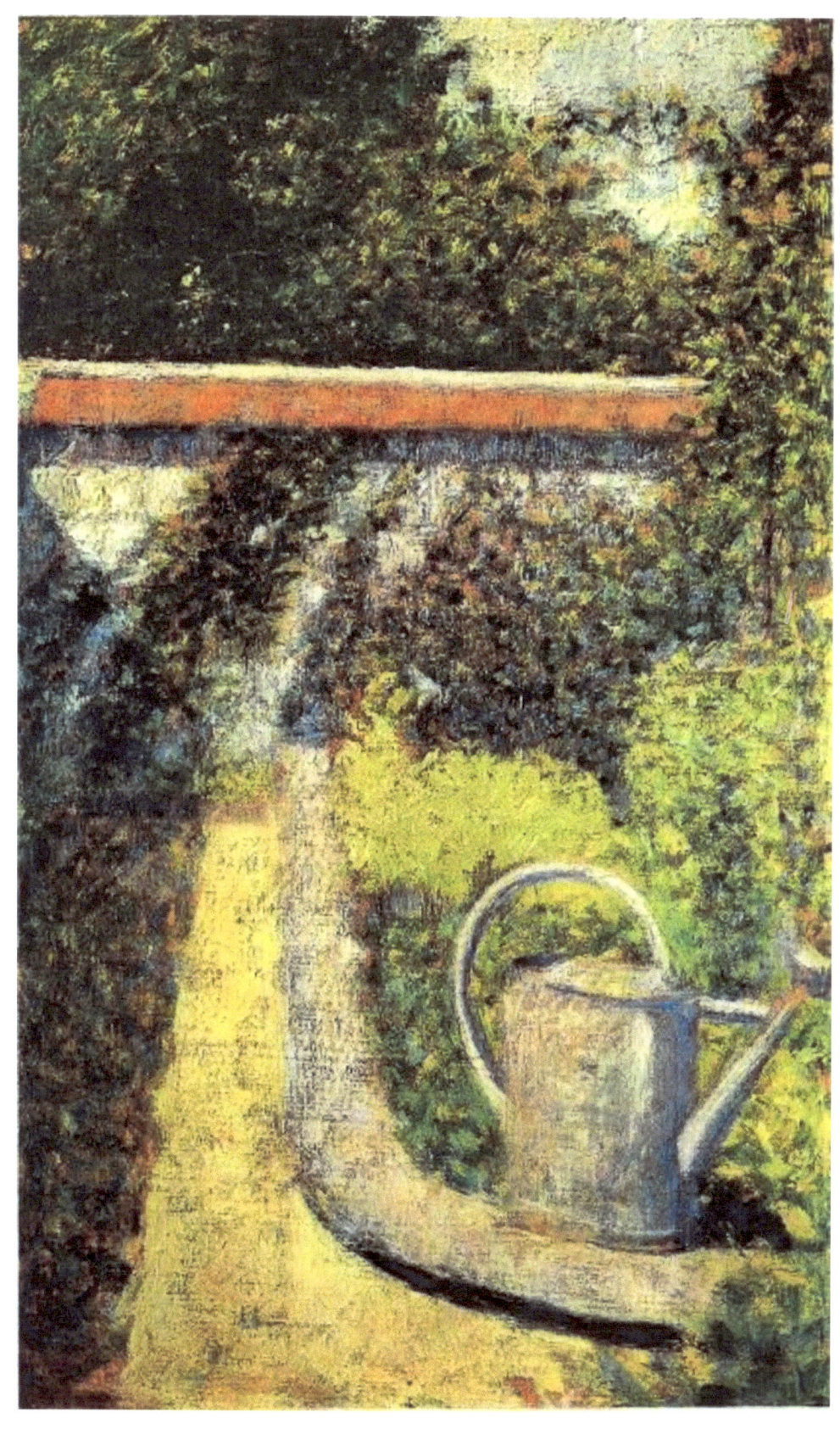

The Watering Can, 1883, oil on wood

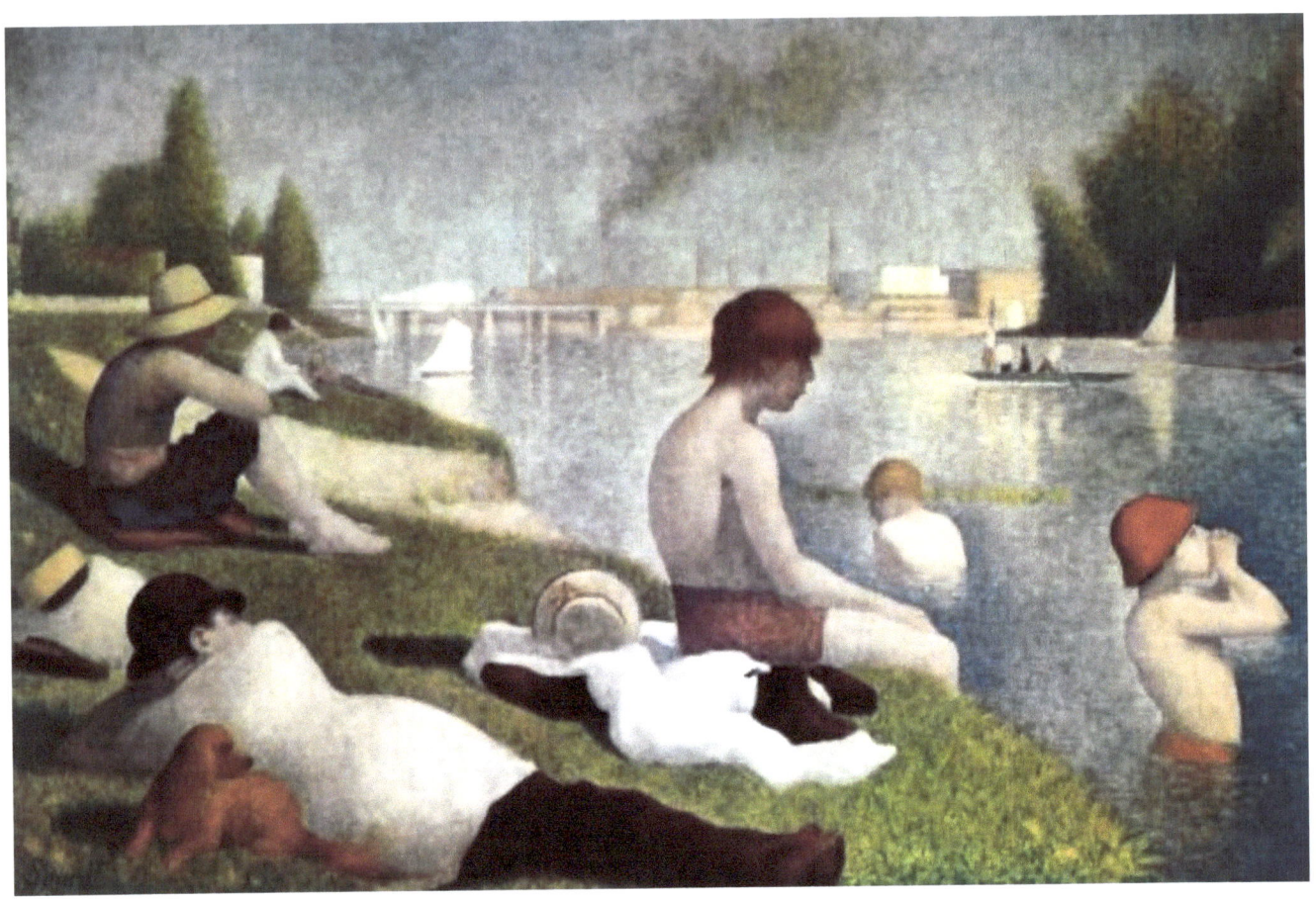

Bathers at Asnieres
1883-84, Oil on canvas, 201 x 300 cm

The Bathers at Asnieres, at two by three metres a demonstratively large work, was Seurat's first programmatic picture. The location was not far out, like Argenteuil or Bougival, but close to newly built factories. There was no restaurant, and those who bathed there went because the rail fare to Argenteuil was too expensive. Fourteen surviving oil studies and a number of drawings show how meticulously Seurat prepared the painting. The atmosphere one of hazy brightness, the sky and water almost constitute a single colour continuum, which powerfully diminishes the spatiality of the work. The figures look exhausted, their three-dimensionality has an inflated look, and the outlines of the colour zones are sharp. These outlines are not marked by actual lines, though, but solely by the different colours of tiny brush-strokes or by an aura of light.

The scientifically precise rendering of colours of this carefree genre scene and sunny landscape admittedly introduces a disquieting note of ornamentality, involving as it does the uncompromising use of a technique that has no time for unimportant details.

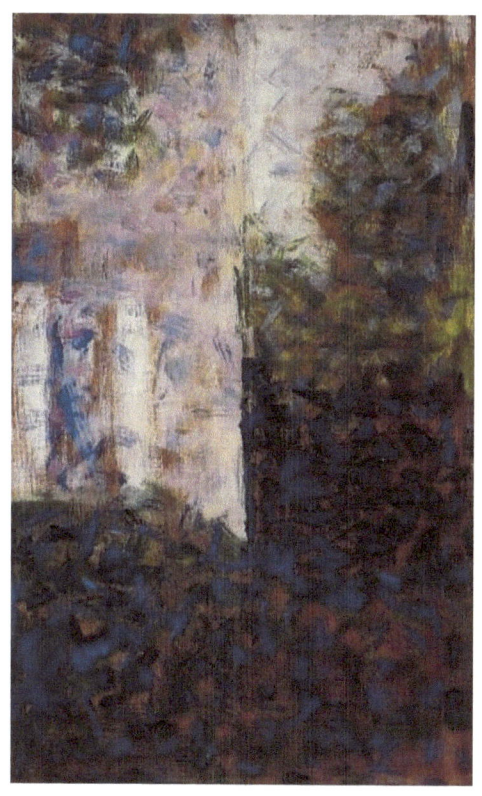

Corner of a House, 1884, oil on canvas

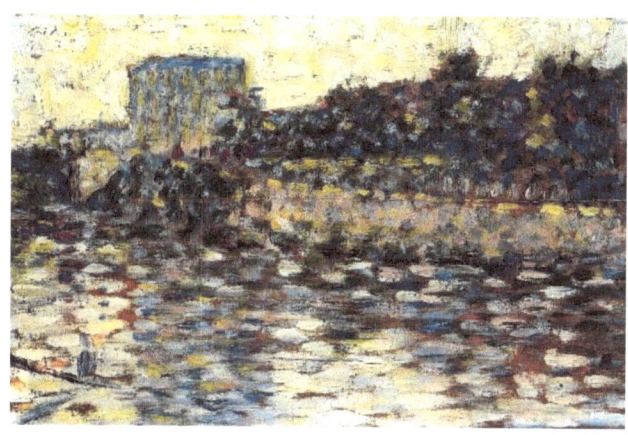

Courbevoie, Landscape With Turret, 1883-1884, oil on wood

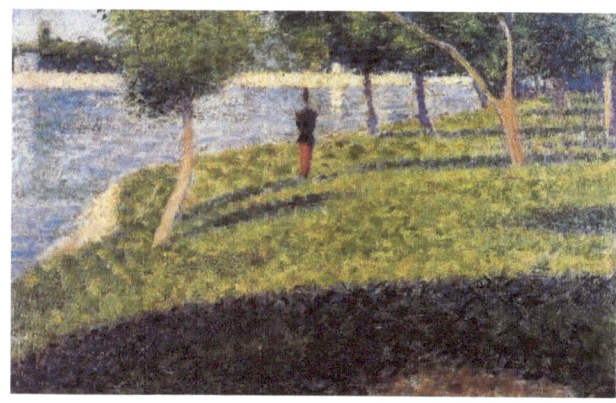

Cadet From Saint-Cyr, 1884, oil on wood

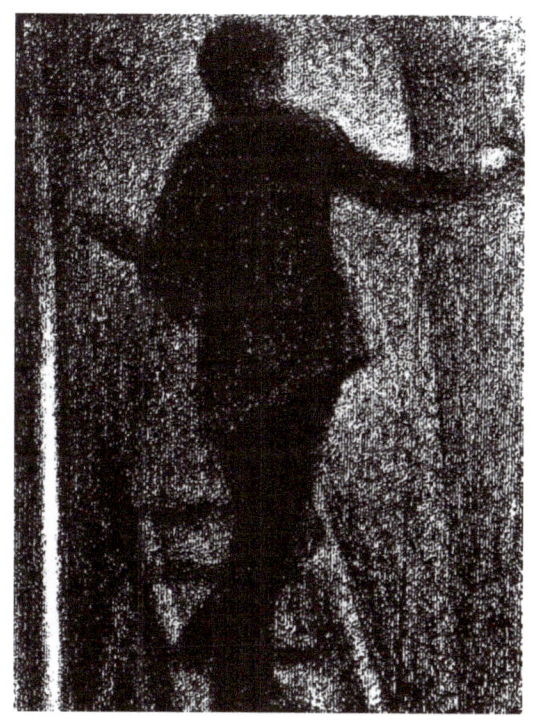

Artist at work, 1884, crayon

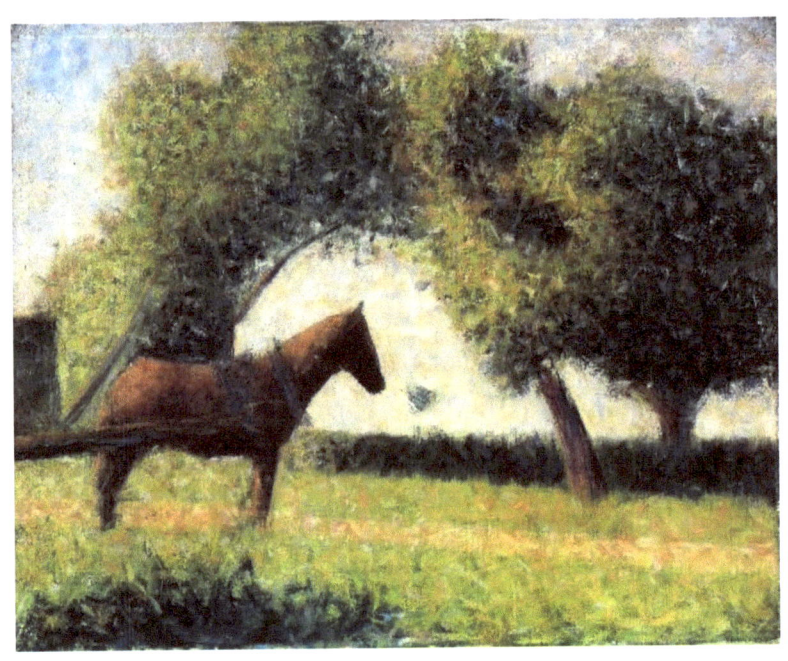

Horse and cart, 1882-1884, oil on canvas

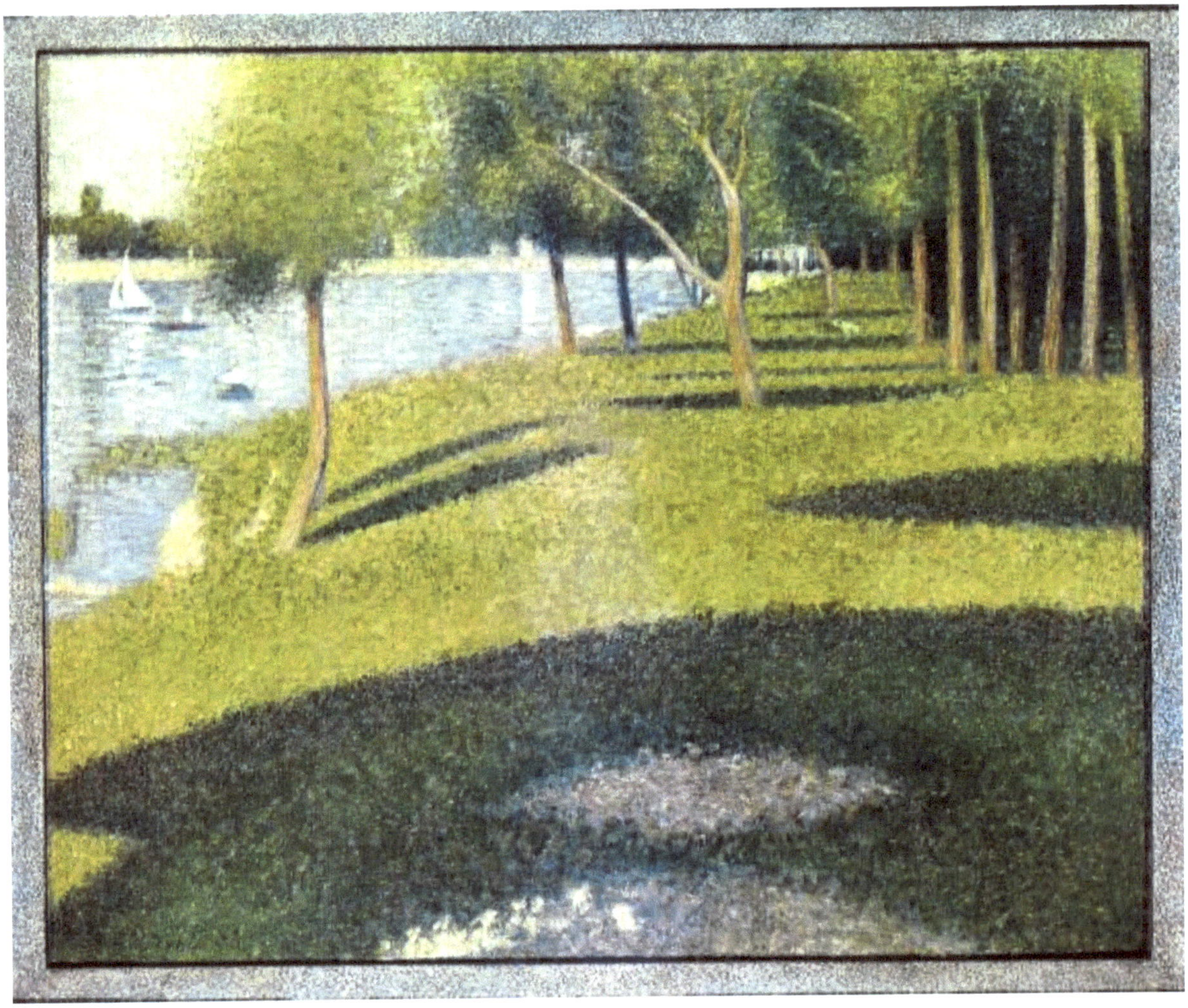

La Grande Jatte, 1884, oil on canvas

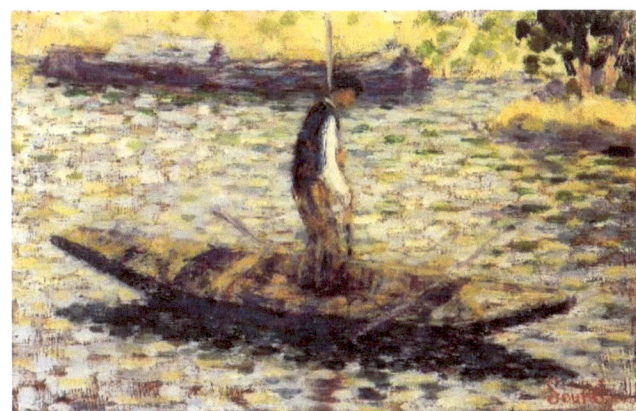

Riverman, 1883-1884, oil on wood

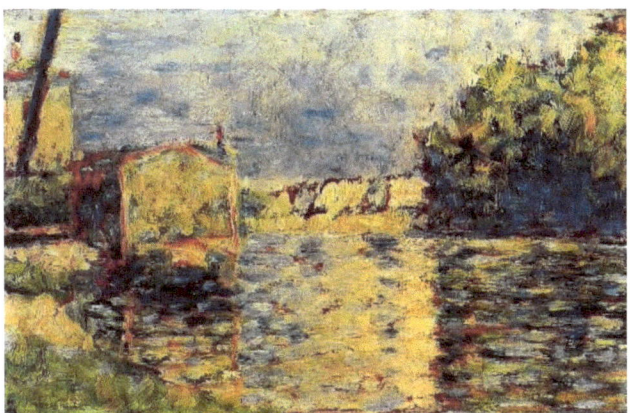

River's Edge, 1883-1884, tempera on canvas

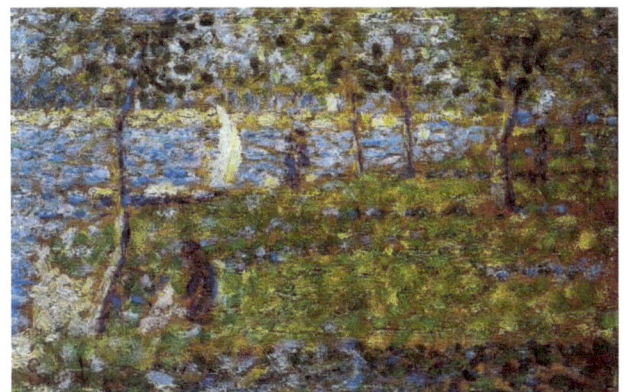

Sailboat, 1884, oil on wood

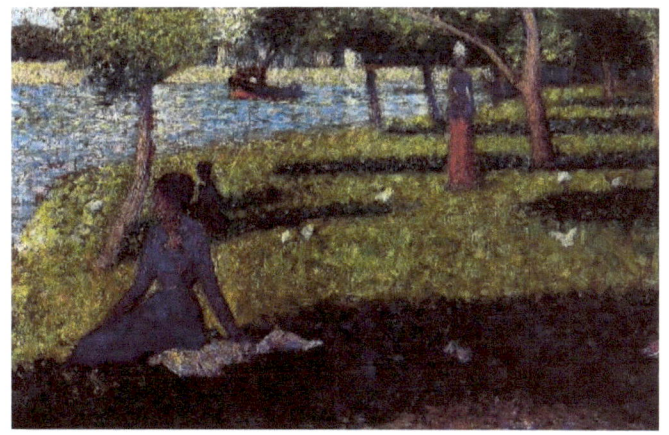

Seated and Standing Woman, 1884, oil on wood

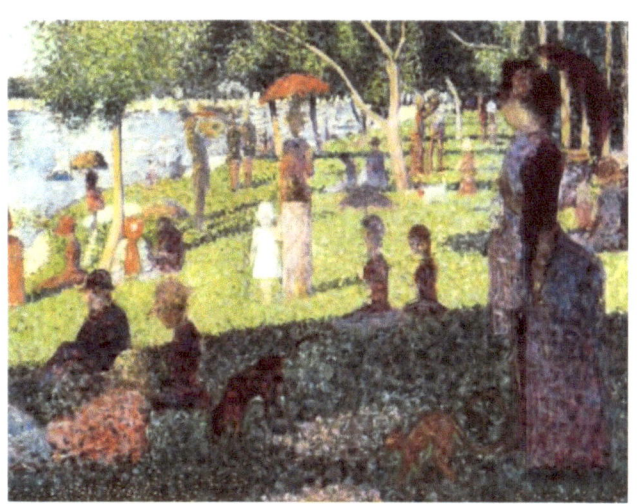

Sketch with Many Figures for Sunday Afternoon on Grande Jatte, 1884, oil on wood

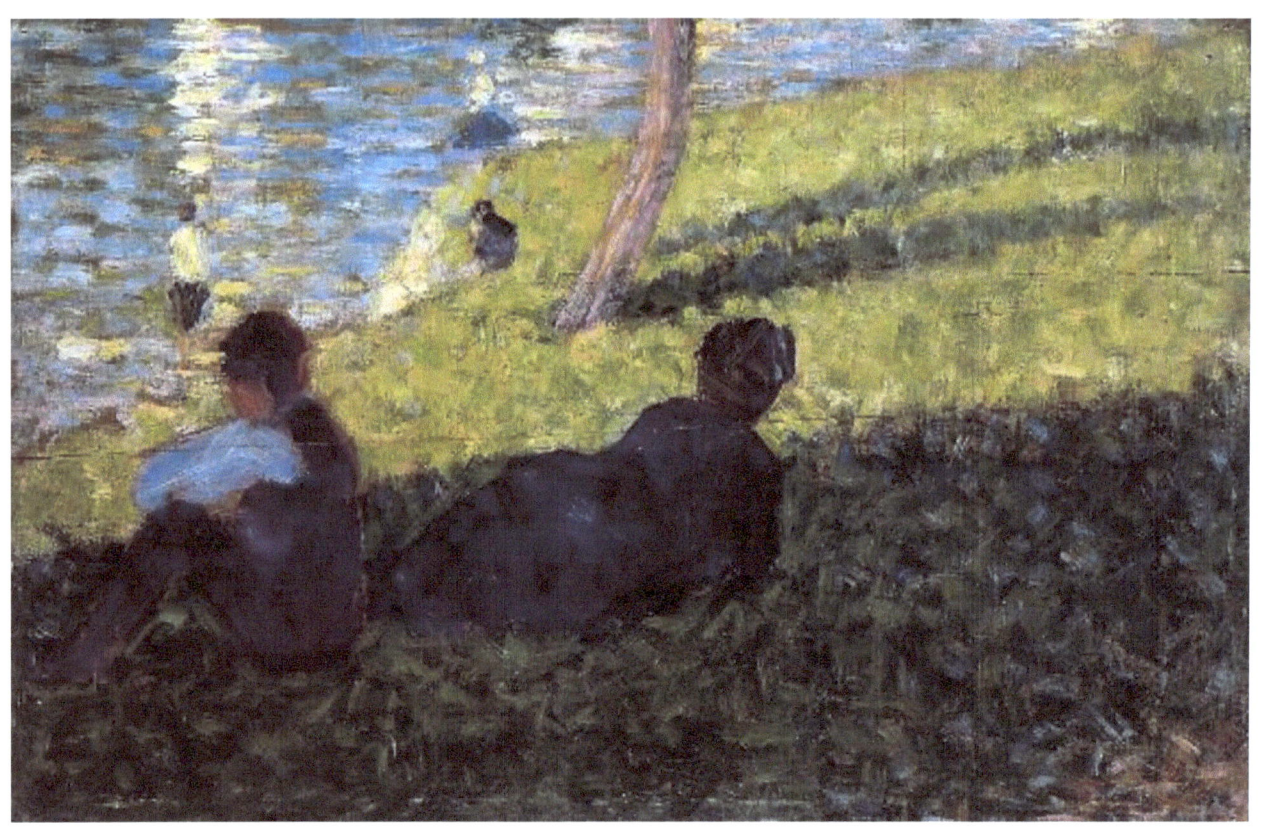

Study for "Un dimanche après midi à l'île de la Grande Jatte", 1884, oil on wood

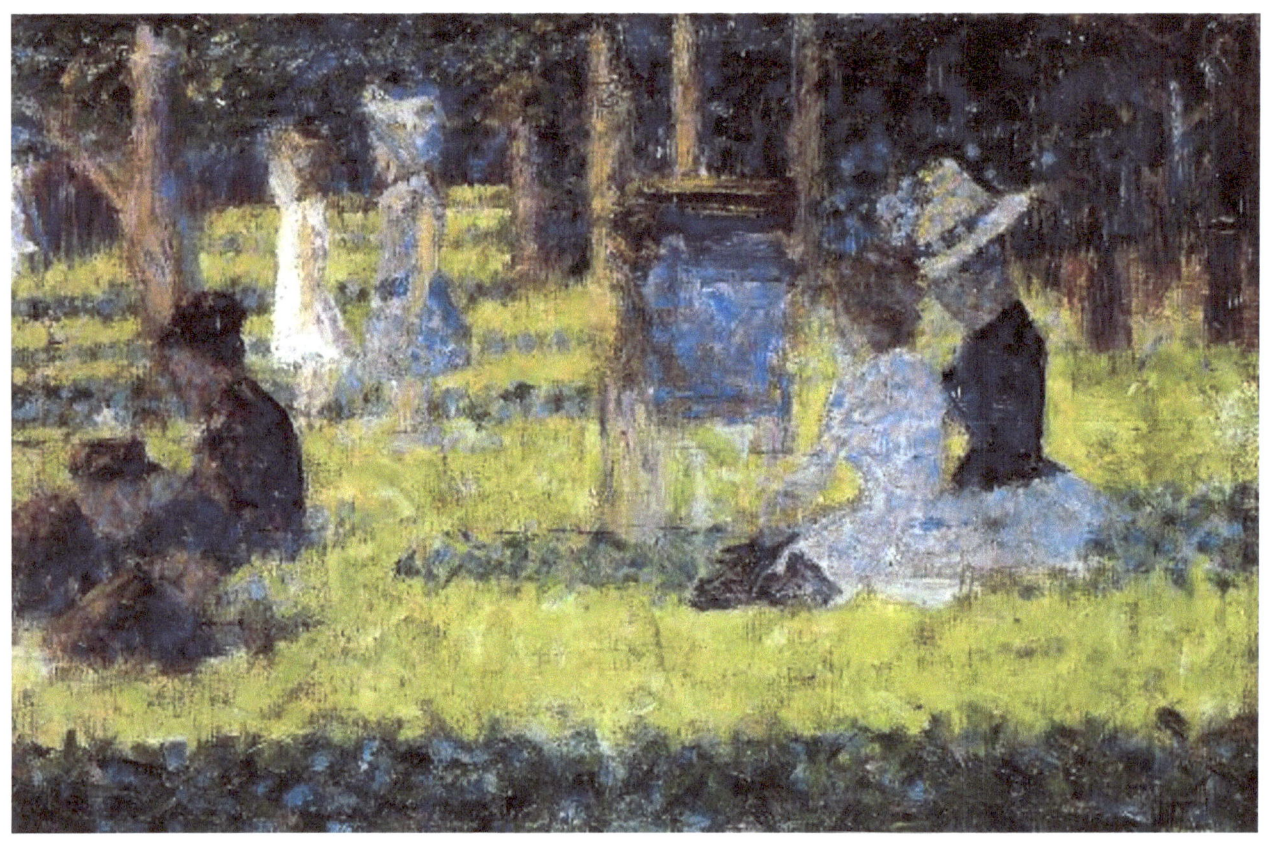

Study for 'A Sunday Afternoon on the Island of La Grande Jatte', 1884, oil on canvas

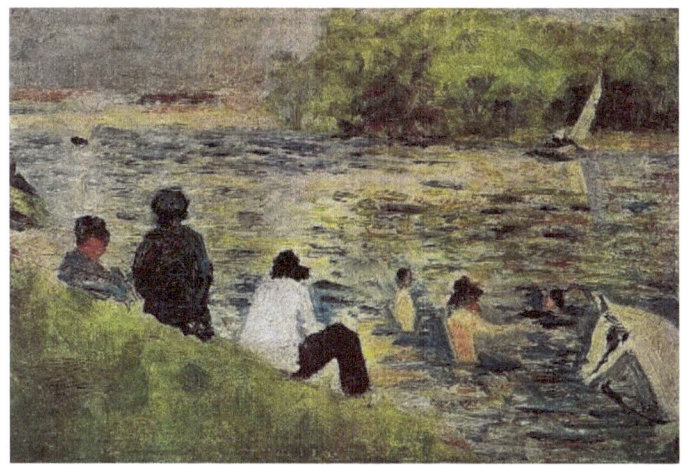

The Bank of the Seine, 1883-1884, oil on wood

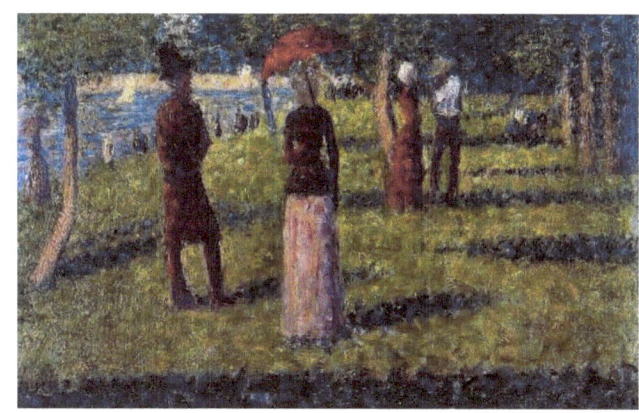

The Rope-Colored Skirt, 1884, oil on wood

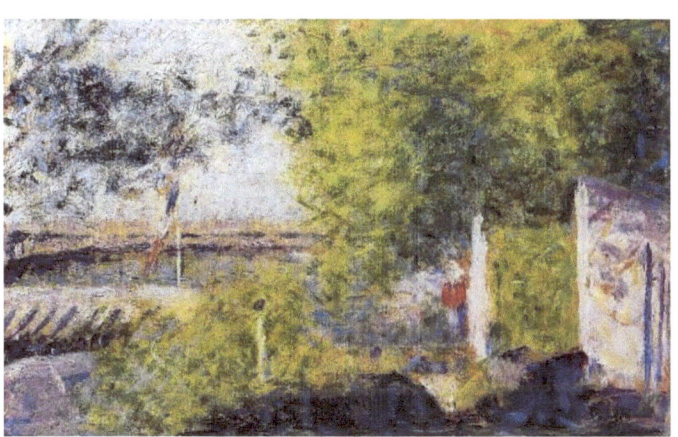

The Bineau Bridge, 1884, oil on wood

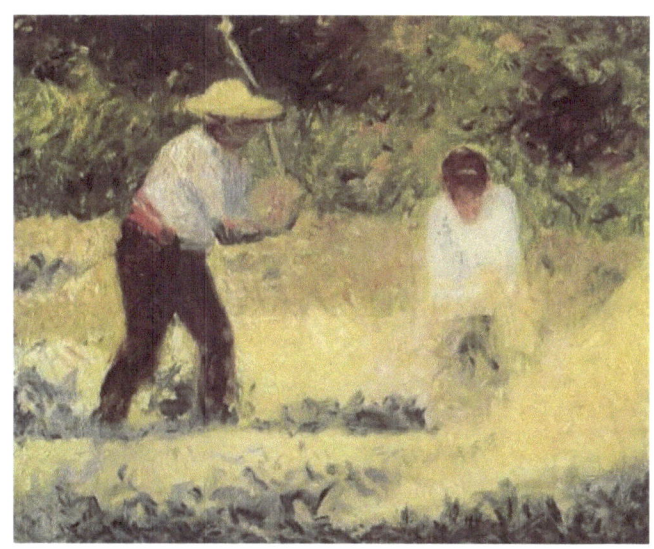

The Stone Breaker, 1884, oil on canvas

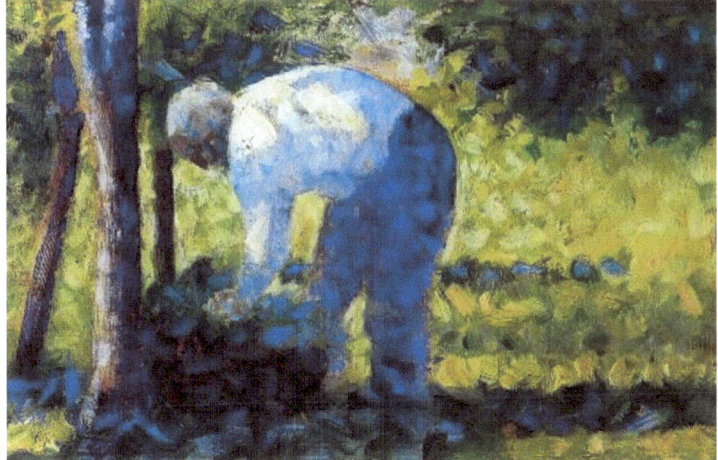

The Gardener, 1883-1884, oil on wood

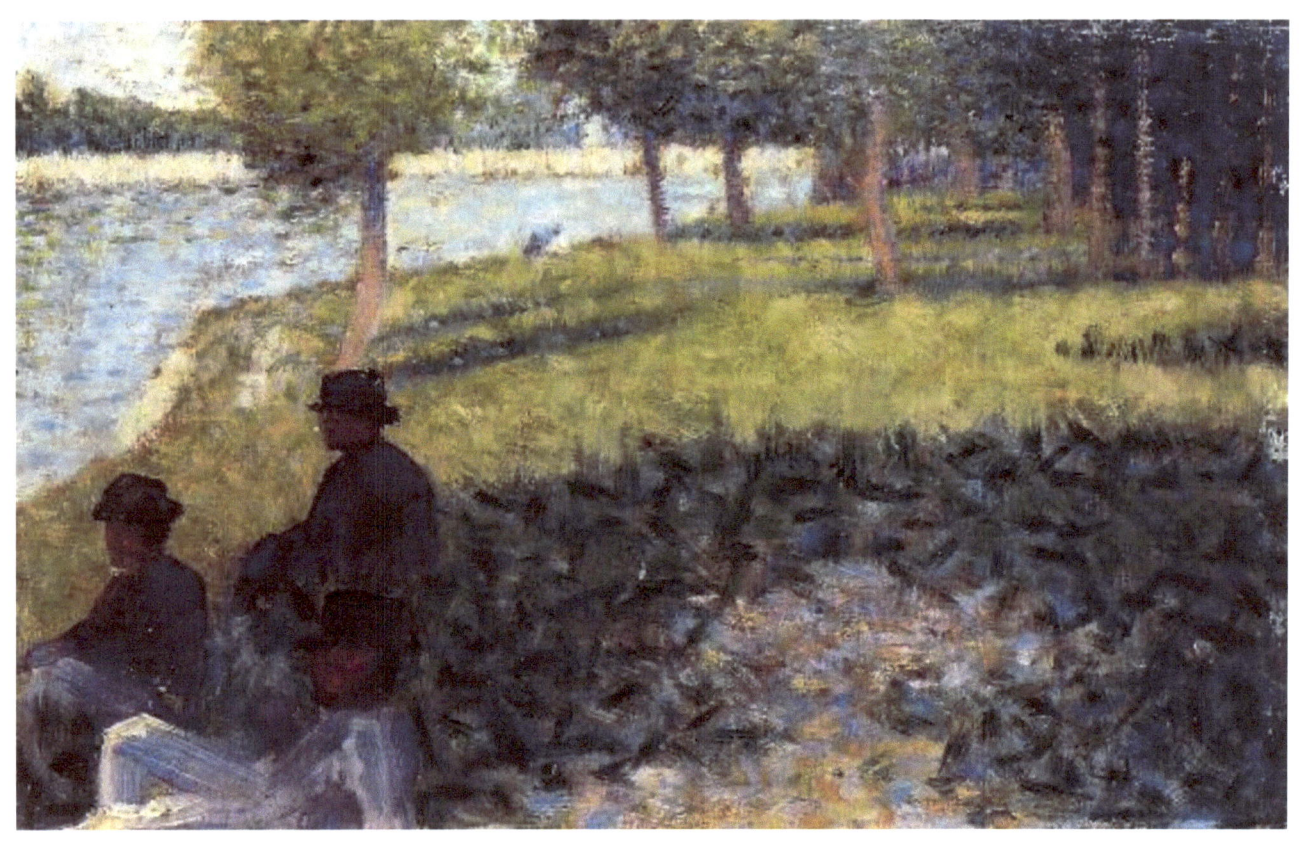

Three Men Seated, 1884, oil on wood

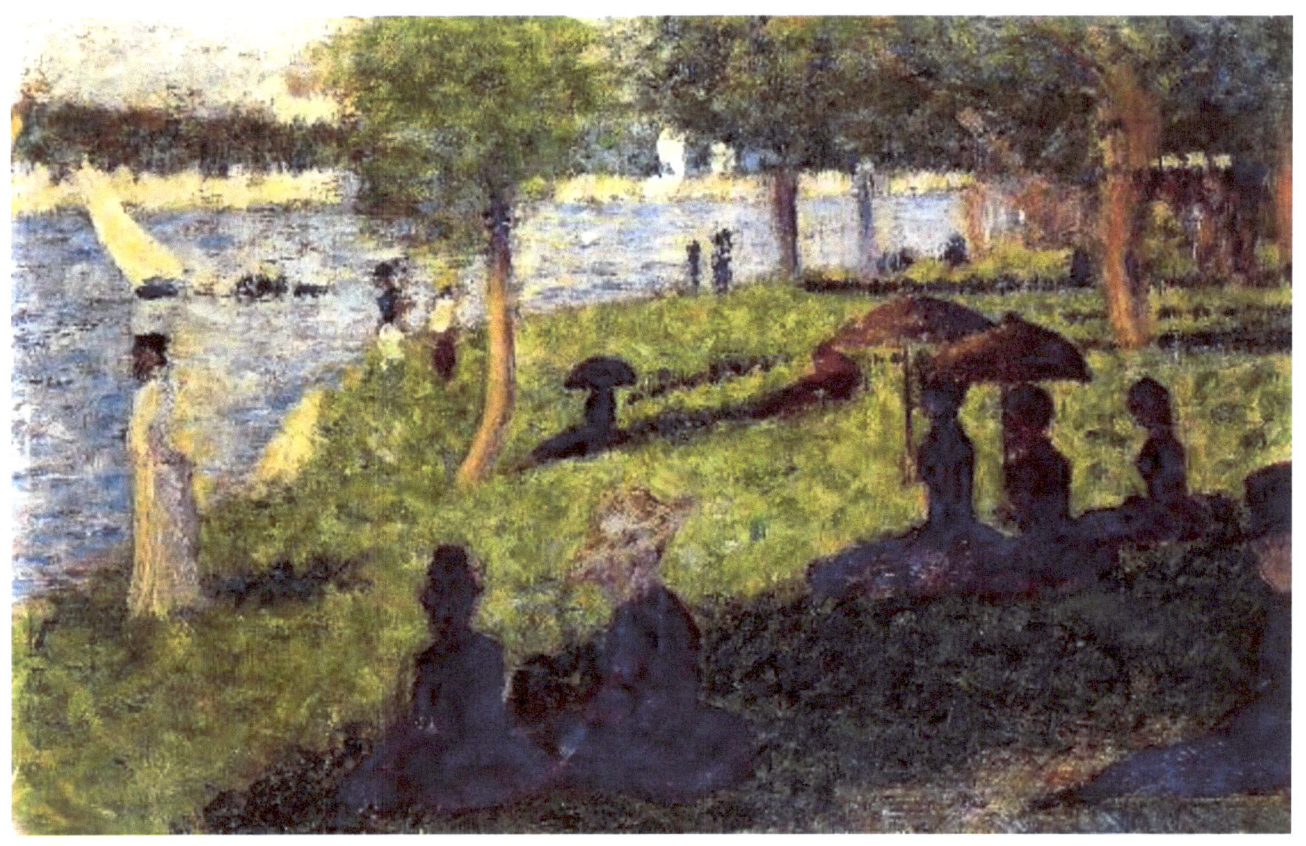

Woman Fishing and Seated Figures, 1884, oil on wood

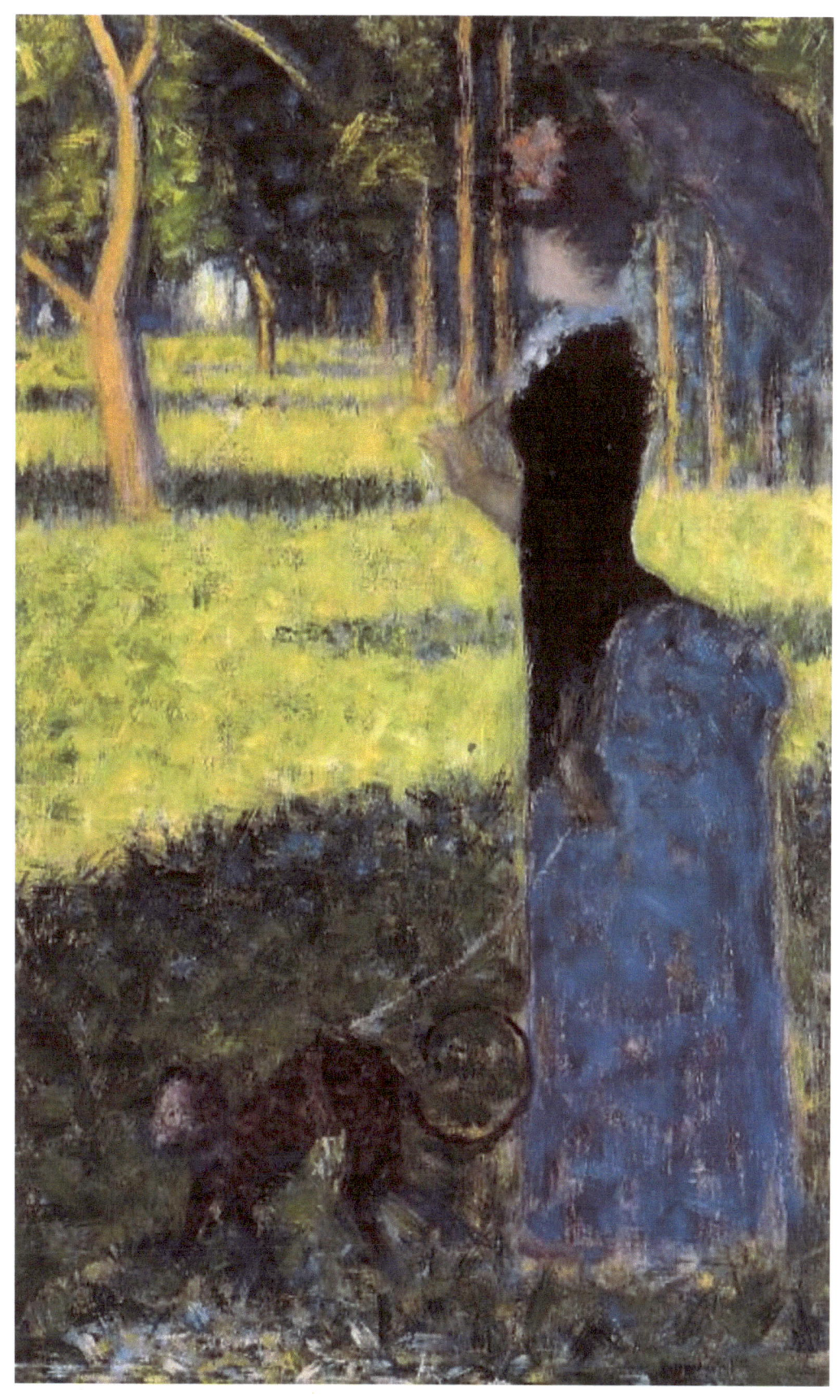

Woman with a Monkey, 1884, oil on wood

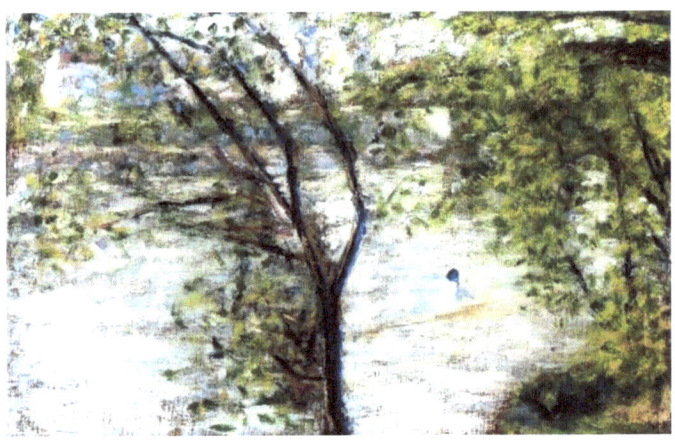

A canoes, 1884-1885, oil on wood

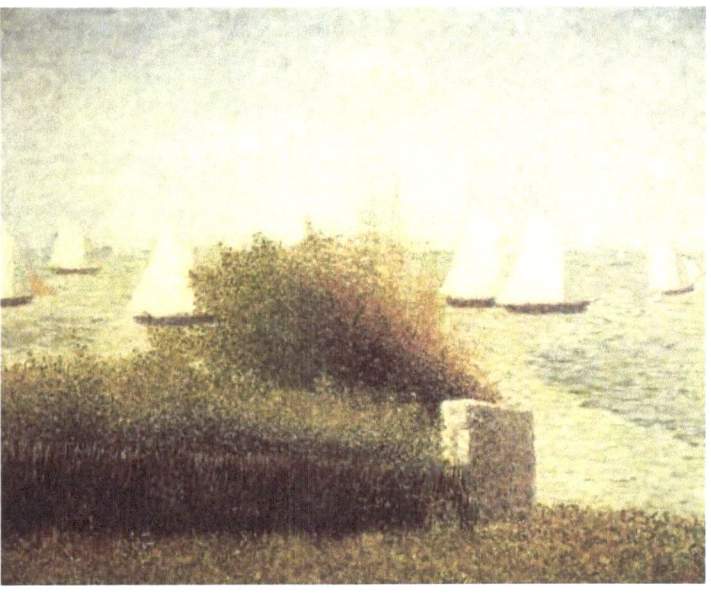

Race in Grandcamp, 1885, oil on canvas

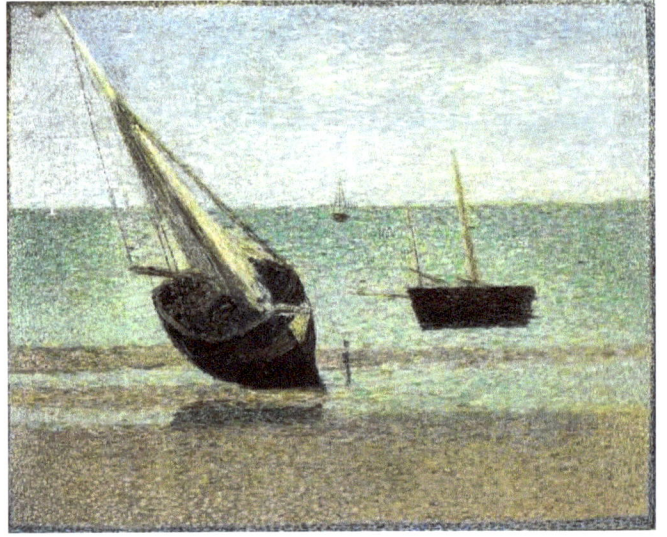

Low Tide at Grandcamp, 1885, oil on canvas

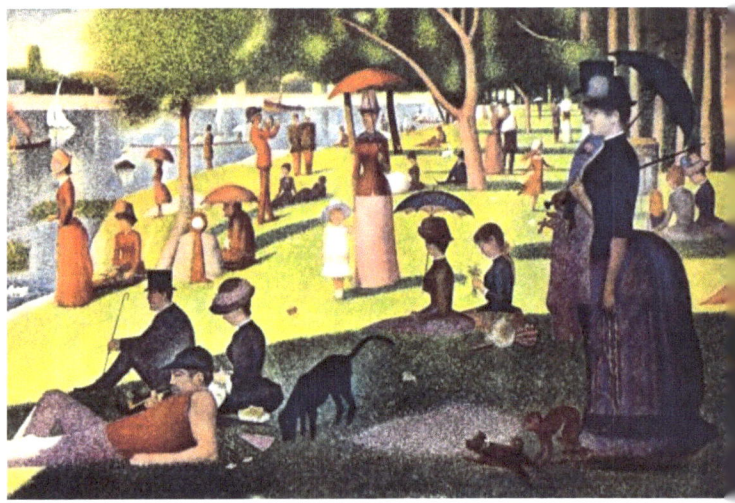

Study for "A Sunday on La Grande Jatte",
1884-1885, oil on canvas

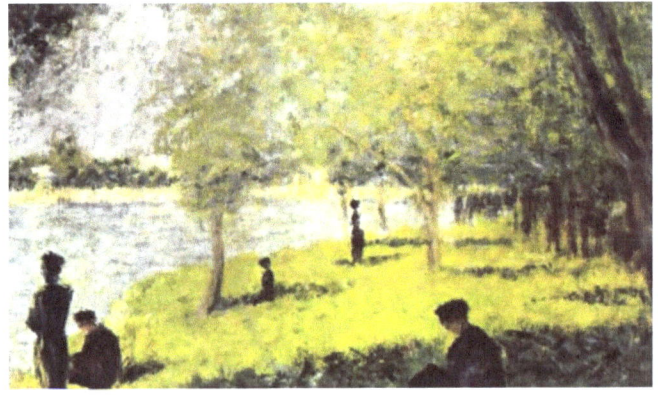

Study with Figures. Study for 'La Grande Jatte', 1884-1885, oil on canvas

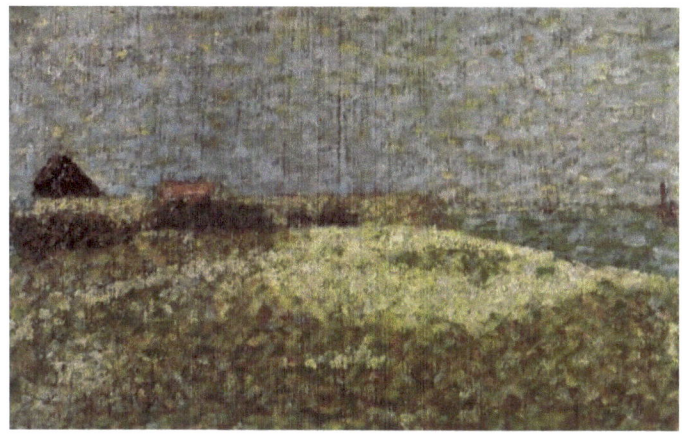

The away Samson in Grandcamp, 1885, oil on wood

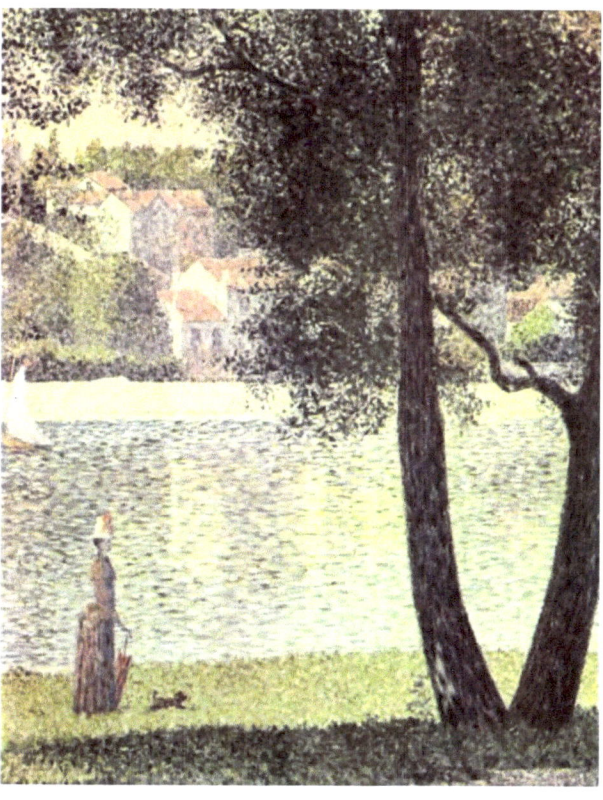

The Seine at Courbevoie, 1885, oil on canvas

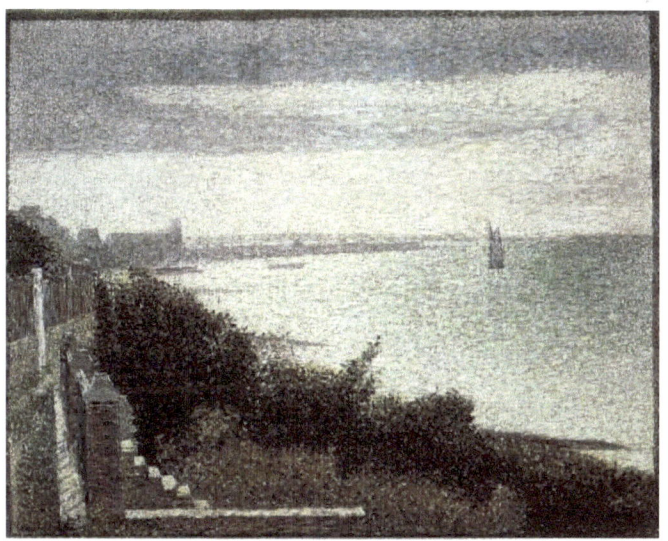

The English Channel at Grandcamp, 1885, oil on canvas

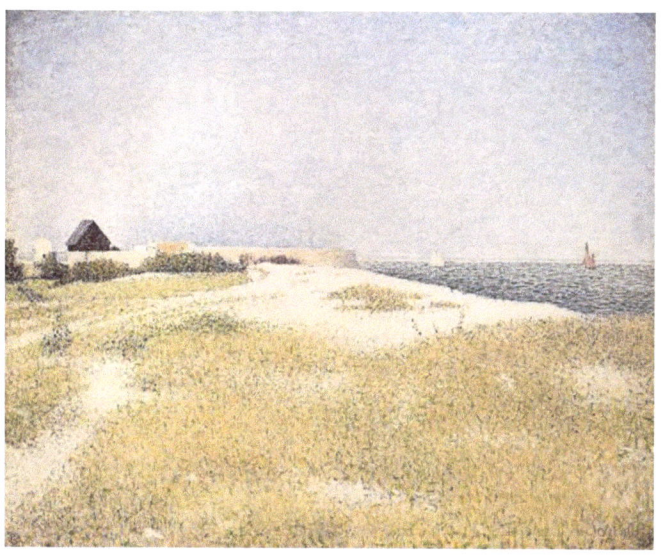

View of Fort Samson, 1885, oil on canvas

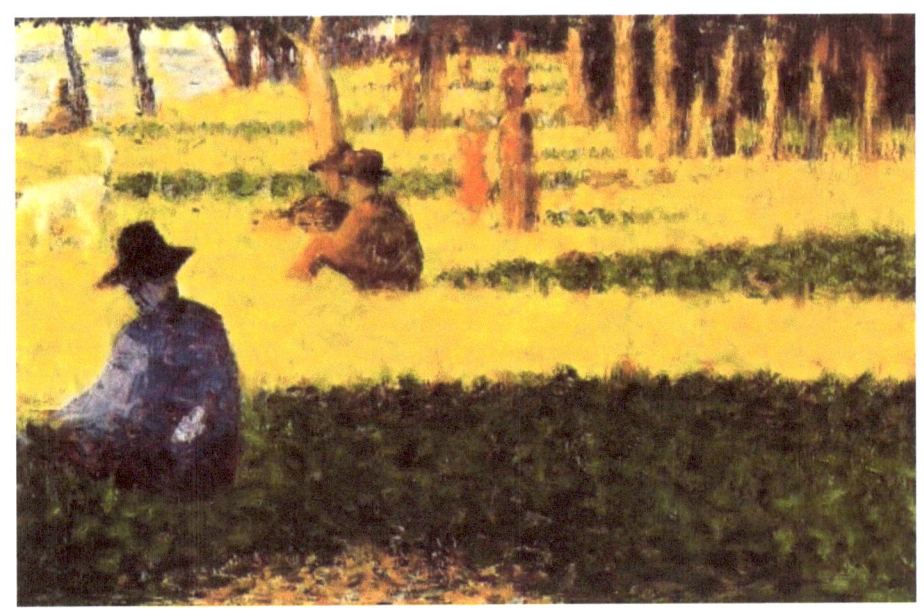

White dog, 1884-1885, oil on wood

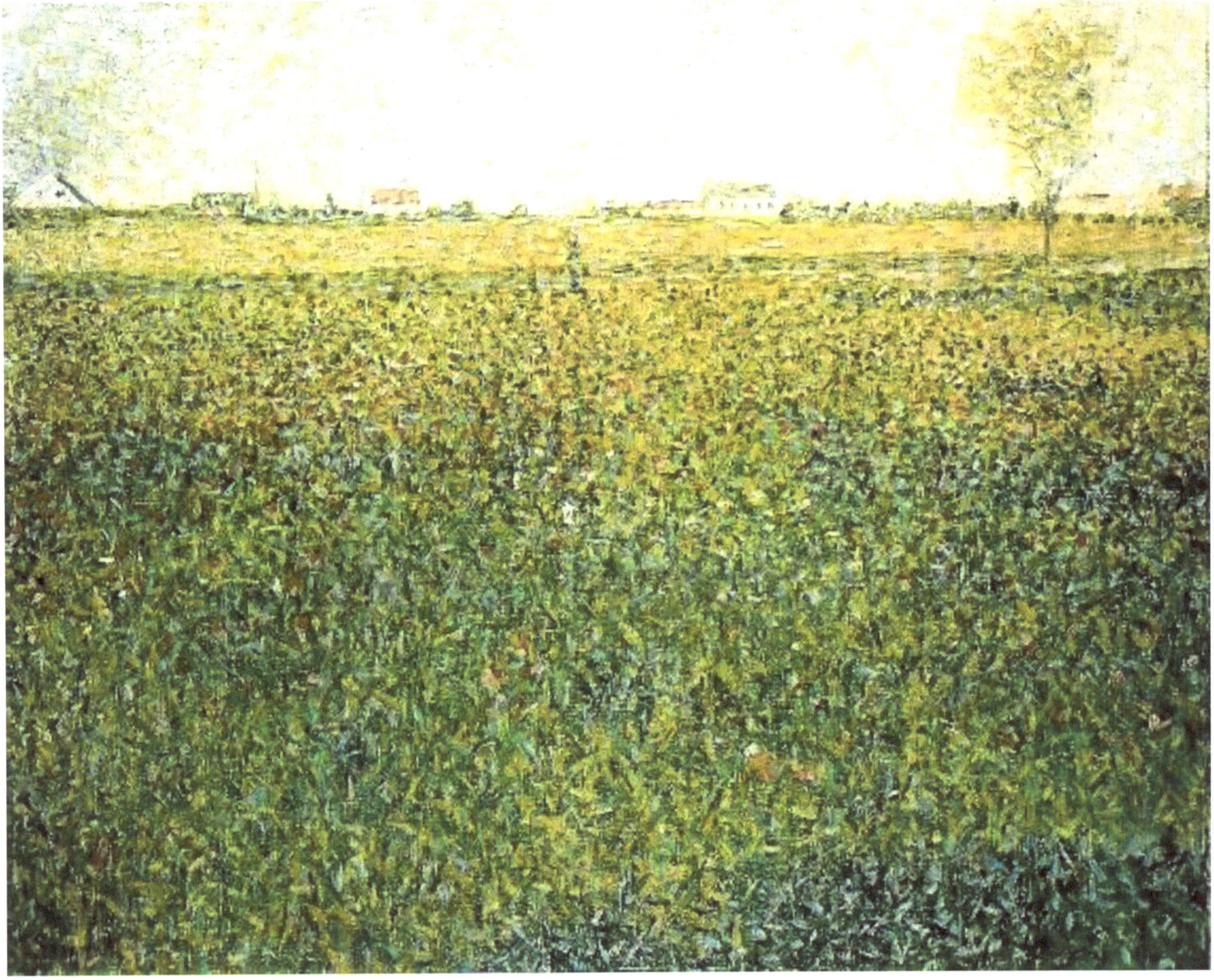

Alfalfa, St. Denis, 1885-1886, oil on canvas

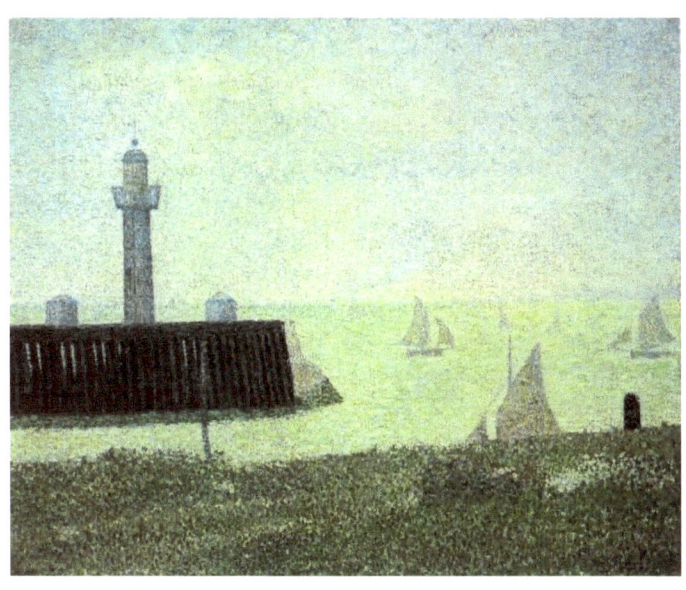

End of the Jetty, Honfleur, 1886, oil on canvas

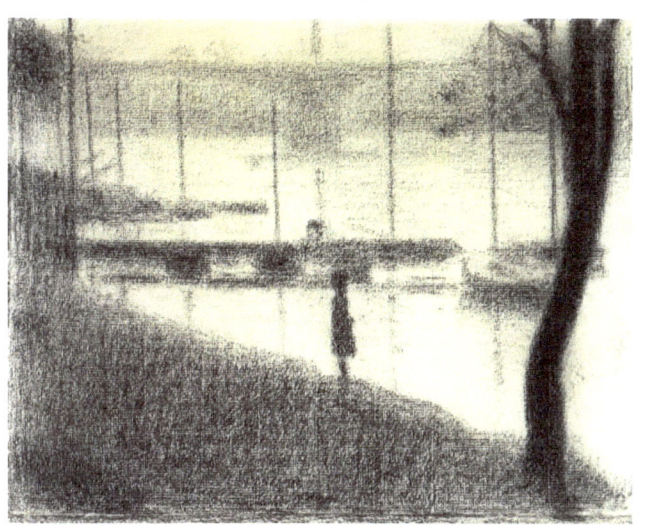

The Pont de Courbevoie, 1886, crayon

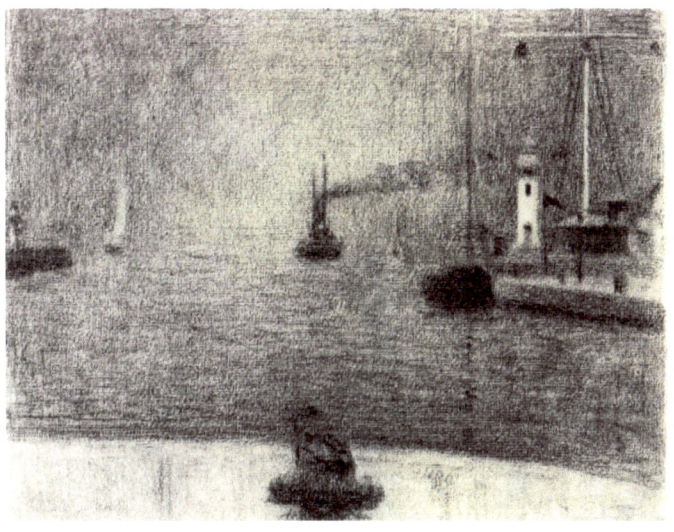

The Port of Honfleur, 1886, crayon

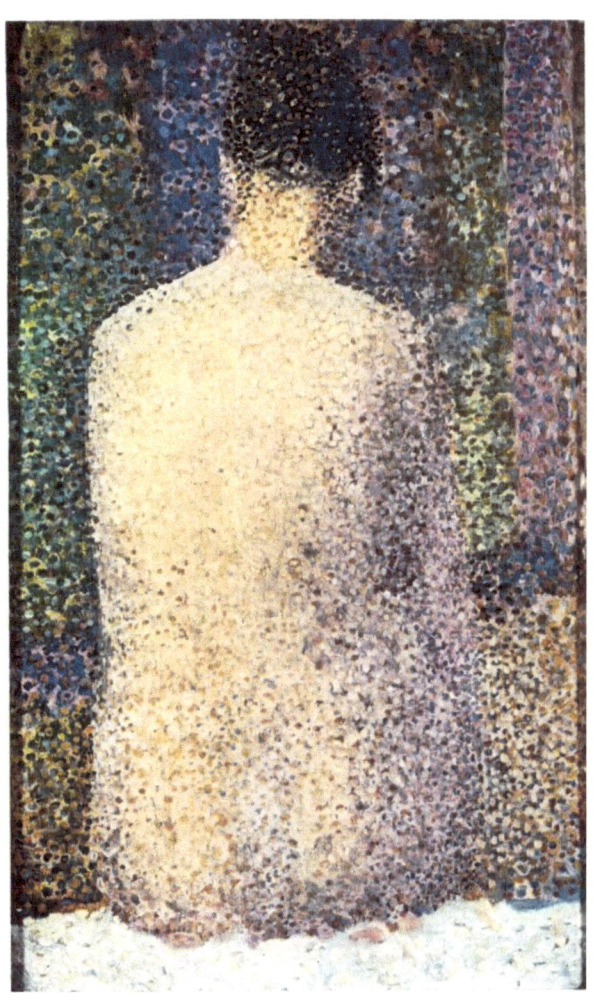

Model from the Back, 1886, oil on wood

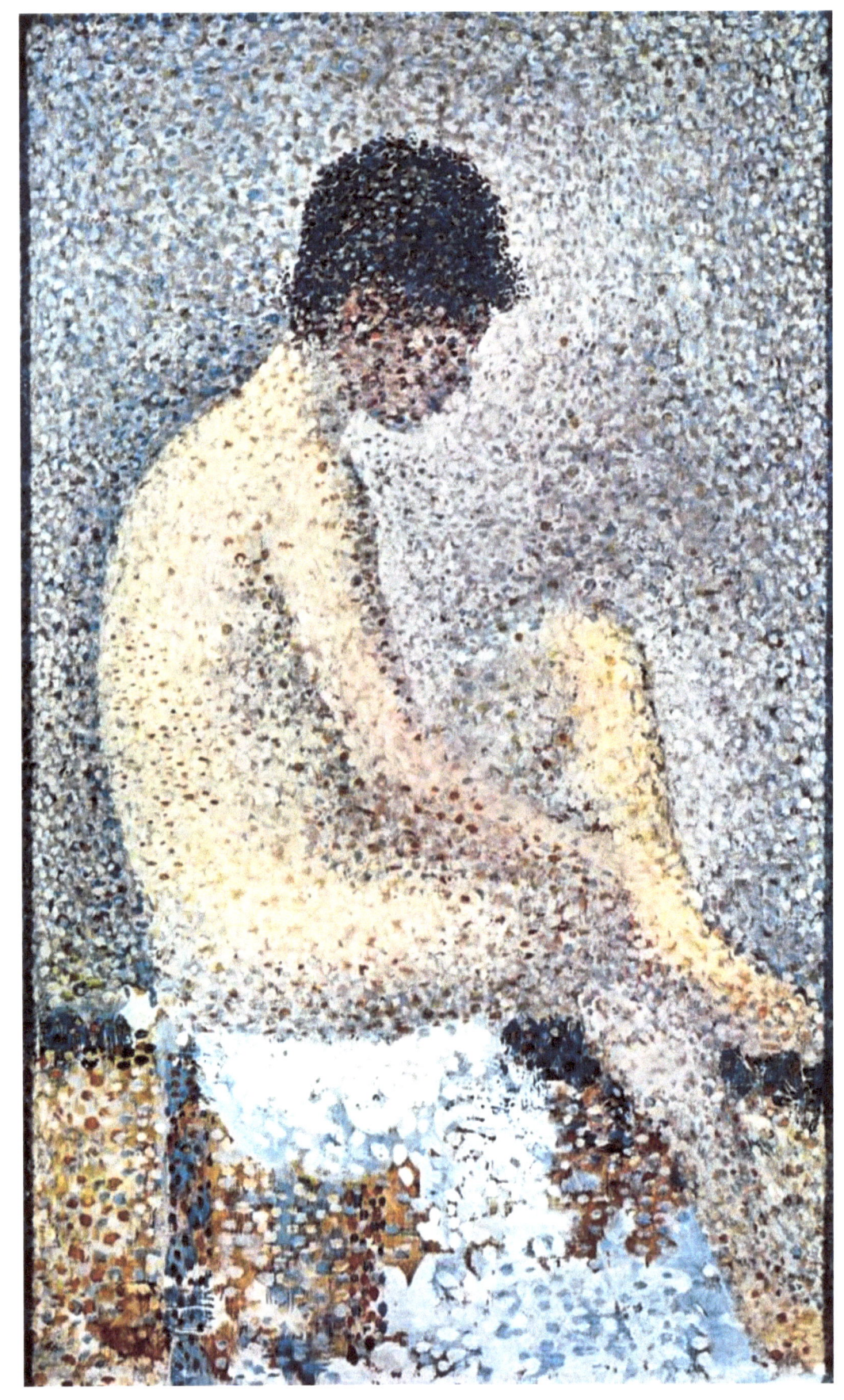

Model in Profile, 1886, oil on wood

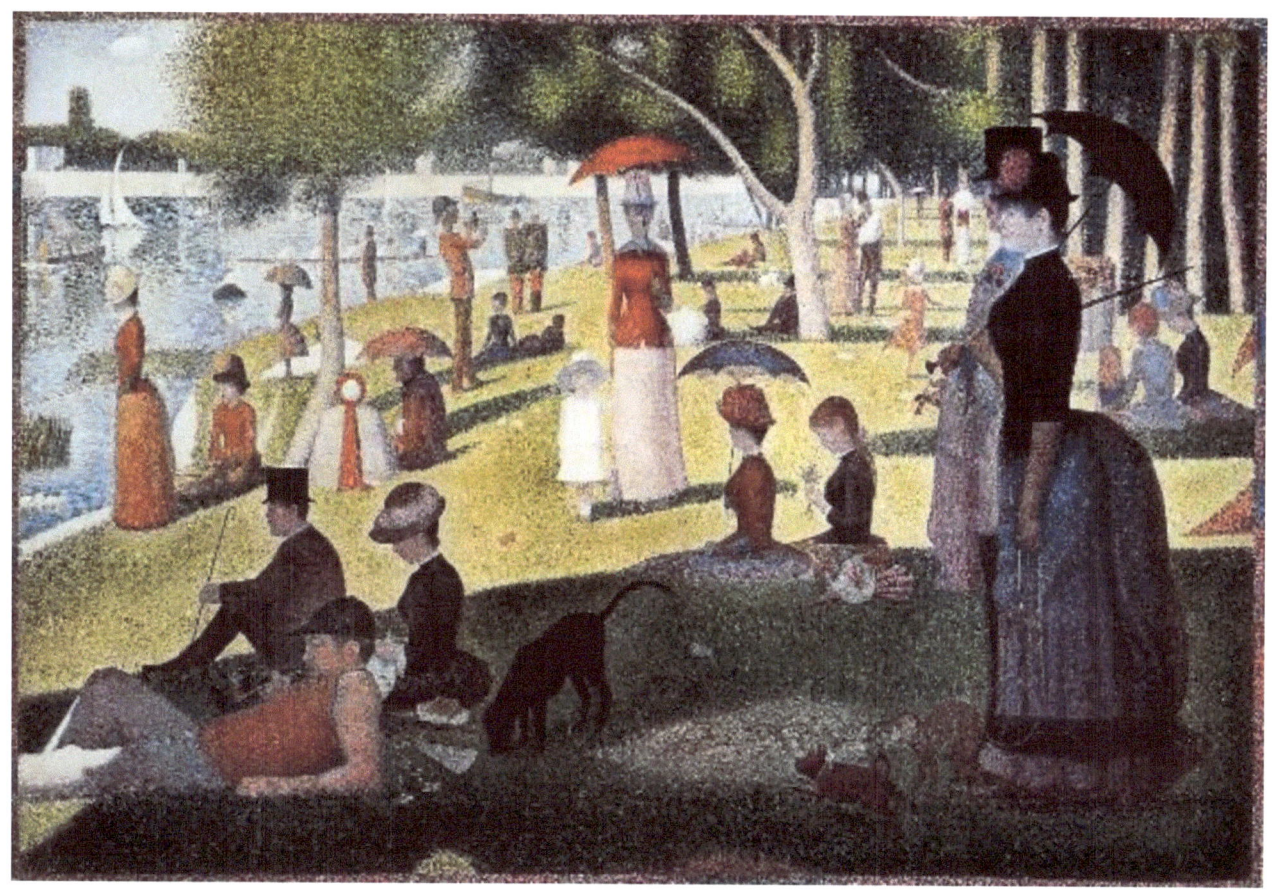

Sunday Afternoon on the Island of La Grande Jatte, 1884-1886, oil on canvas

This painting, shown at the last Impressionist exhibition in 1886, served as the manifesto of Neo-Impressionism. Seurat adopted certain elements of the Impressionist tradition (he made outdoor colour studies and he retained the light tonality of the Impressionist palette), but his training took place well away from the protagonists of modern art, following a highly personal course from the outset. He took up colour by reading scientific books on optical phenomena. In the scientific literature a number of principles were formulated that subsequently formed the theoretical base of Neo-Impressionism: the distinction between hue and tone (or colour and value)), the idea of the optical mixing effected by the retina, and the coloured vibrations obtained by juxtaposing different tones of the same hue.

In Neo-Impressionism the conflict between representation and abstraction was glaring. The tendency to treat figures as coloured silhouettes reached its height in A Sunday Afternoon on the Ile de la Grande Jatte in which "the stiffness of the characters and the incisive shapes help to generate the sound of modernity."

In this best-known and largest painting, Georges Seurat depicted people relaxing in a suburban park on an island in the Seine River called La Grande Jatte. The artist worked on the painting in several campaigns, beginning in 1884 with a layer of small horizontal brushstrokes of complementary colours. He later added small dots, also in complementary colours, that appear as solid and luminous forms when seen from a distance. Seurat made the final changes to La Grande Jatte in 1889. He restretched the canvas in order to add a painted border of red, orange, and blue dots that provides a visual transition between the interior of the painting and his specially designed white frame.

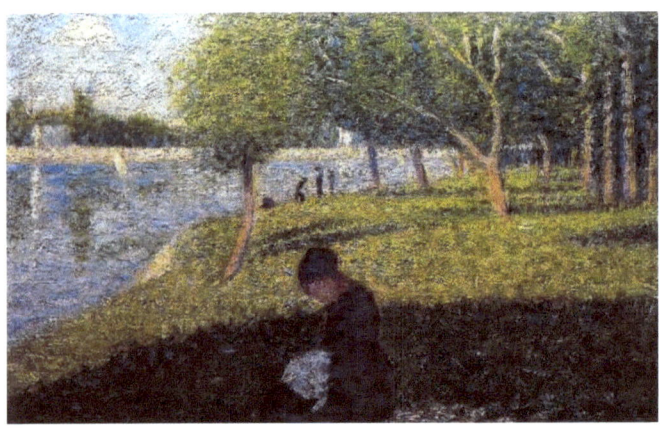

Study for 'A Sunday Afternoon on the Island
of La Grande Jatte', 1884-1886, oil on wood

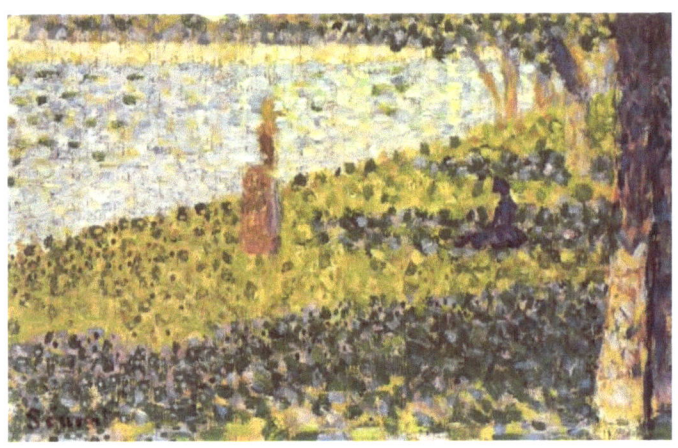

Women by the Water, 1885-1886, oil on
wood

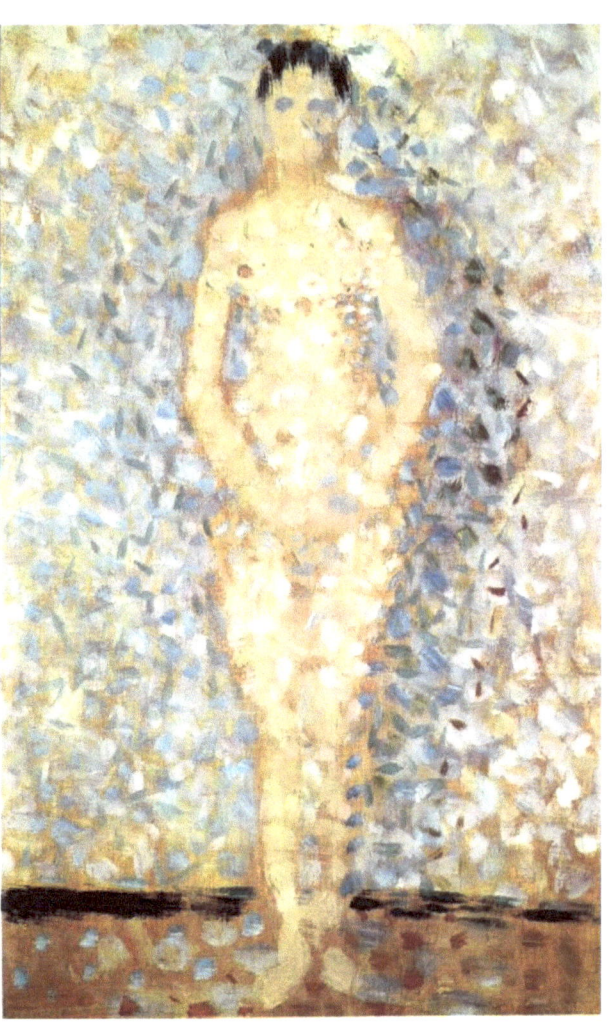

Poseur standing, front view, study for "Les
poseuses", 1887, oil on wood

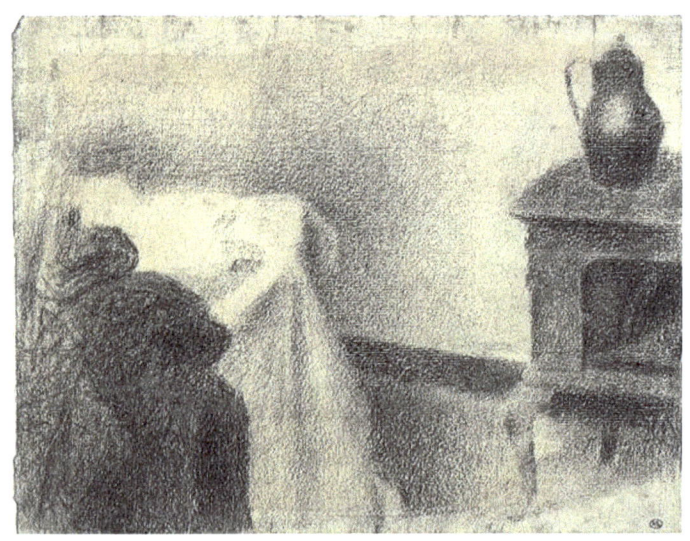

Part of the studio, 1887, crayon

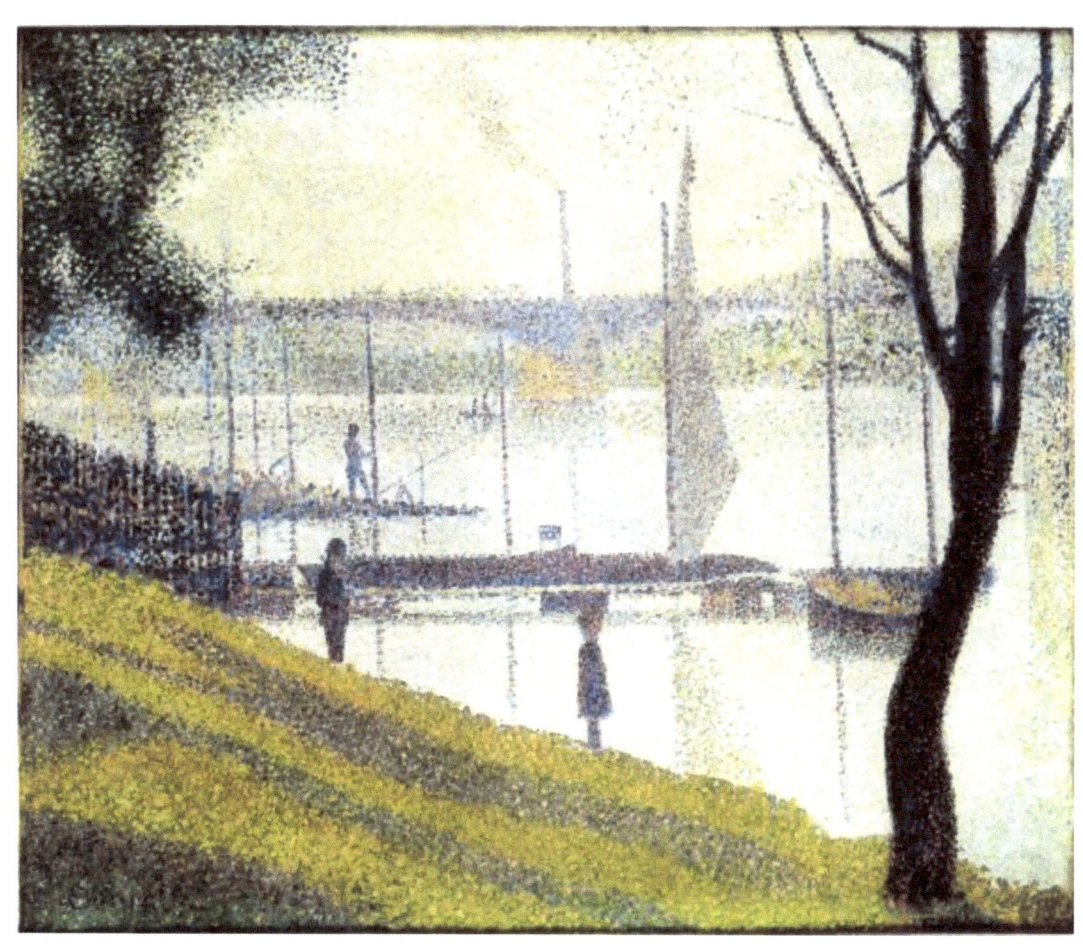

The Bridge at Courbevoie, 1886-1887, oil on canvas

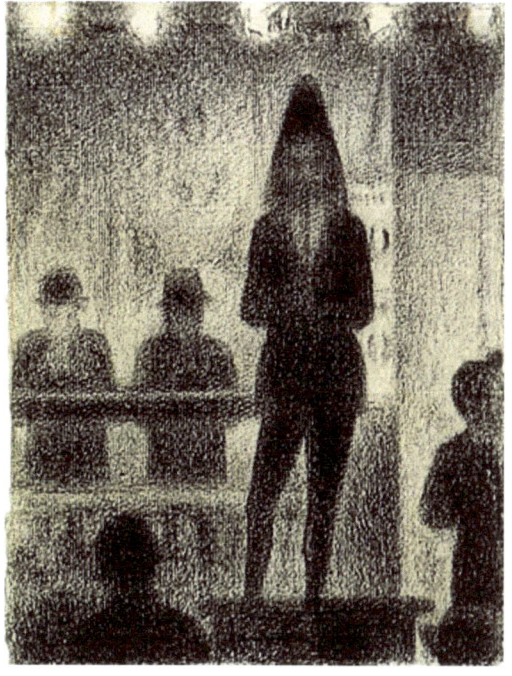

Trombone player, 1887, crayon

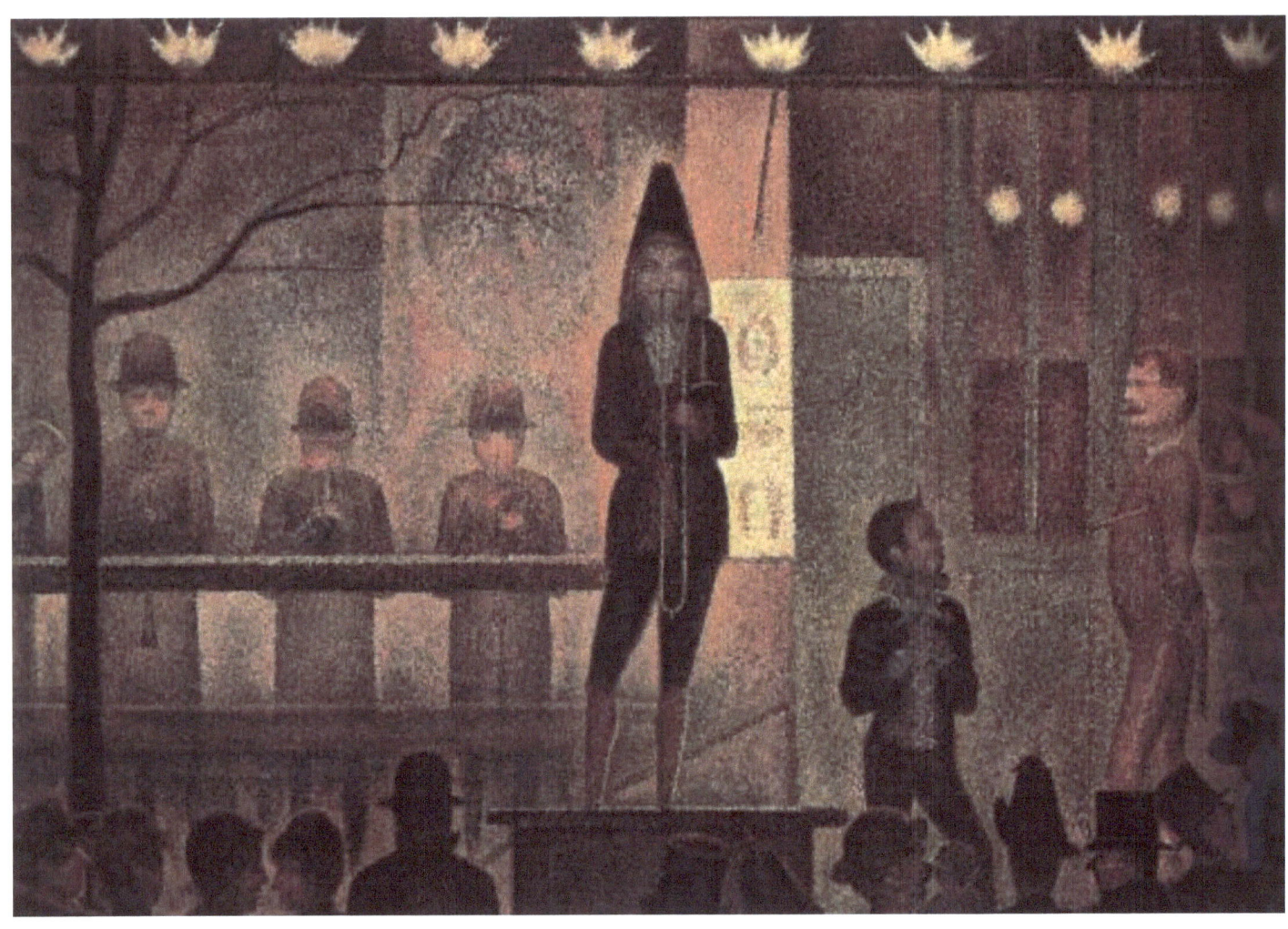

Circus Sideshow, 1887-1888, oil on canvas

In the mid-1880 the depiction of suburban pleasures favoured by the Impressionists gave way to pictures of urban entertainment, as writers, poets, and songwriters turned to acrobats, clowns, and cafñ singers for subject matter. Seurat's interest in urban entertainment culminated in Circus Sideshow. The scene is a sideshow given in the evening on the street to lure passersby into purchasing tickets to the circus. But instead of being gay and festive, the performance is calm and brooding. Using a fine brush, Seurat has covered the canvas with a myriad of dark violet-blue, orange, and green dots of paint. Although his research in optics was purportedly scientific, the forms are endowed with mystery. Figures seem to levitate in the moody gaslight, musicians and performers are eerily geometric and alienated from the audience, and railings suggest ramps that lead nowhere. In this world where nothing is certain to the eye, Seurat implies parity between fact and fantasy.

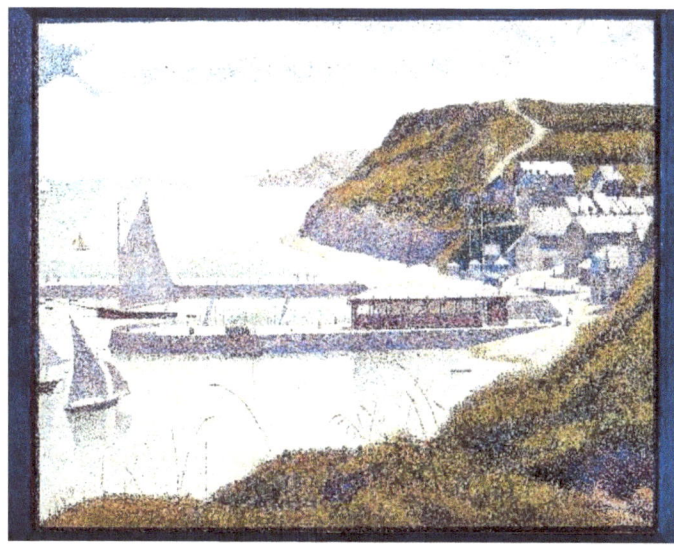

Harbour at Port-en-Bessin at High Tide,
1888, oil on canvas

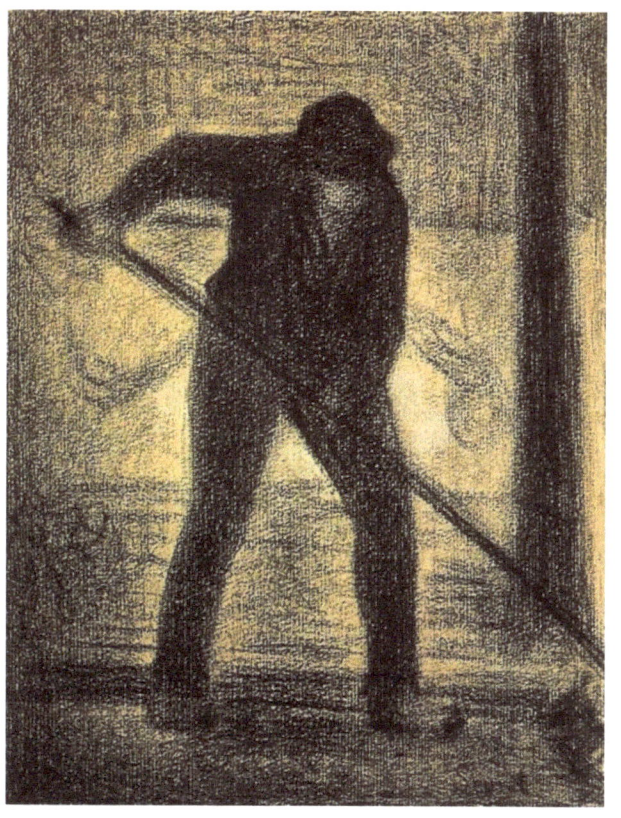

The Garbage Picker, 1888, crayon

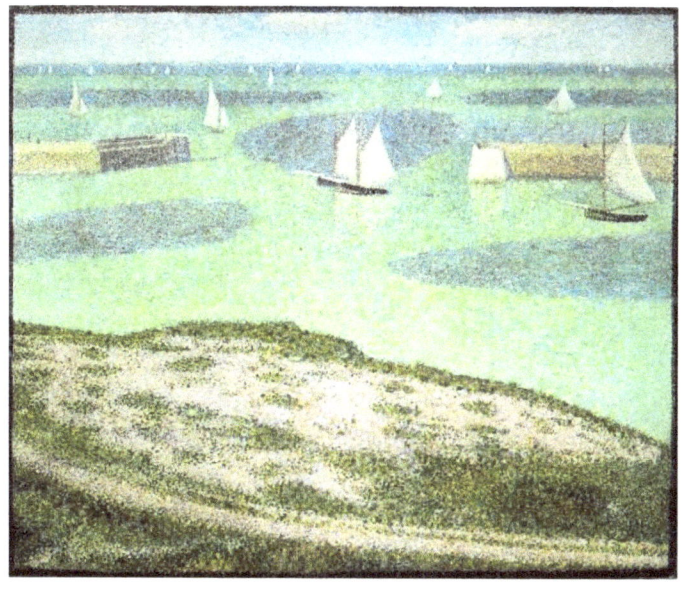

Port-en-Bessin Entrance to the Harbor, 1888,
oil on canvas

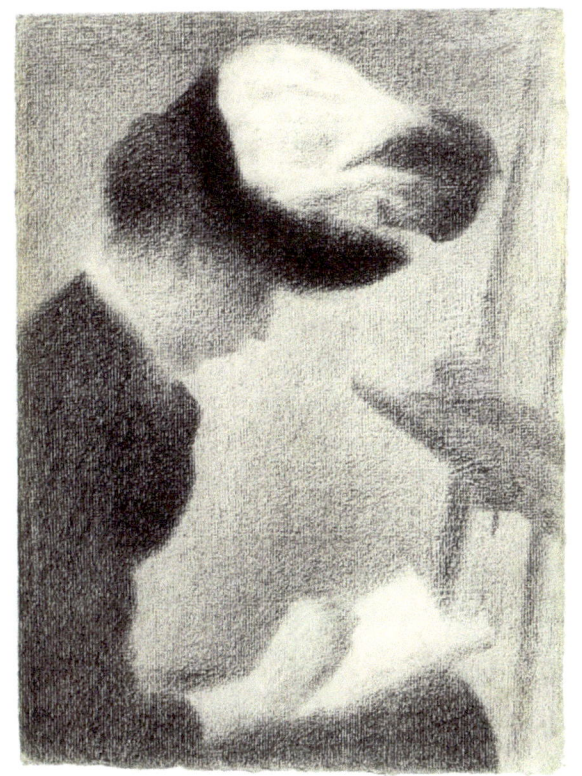

Woman Seated by an Easel, 1888, crayon

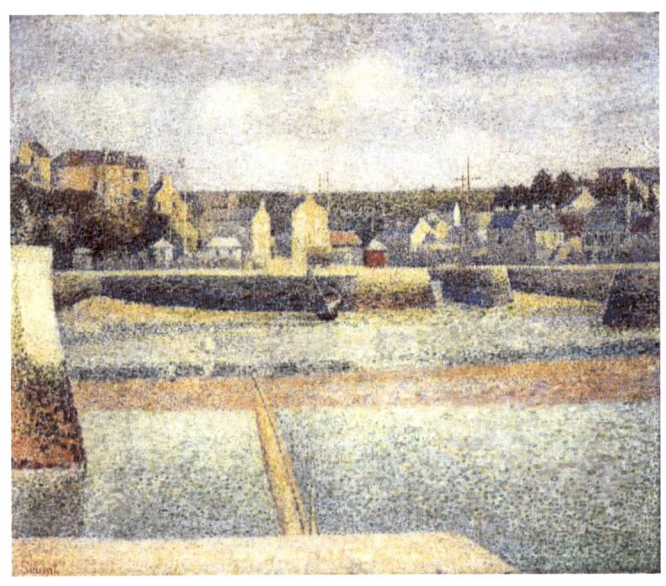

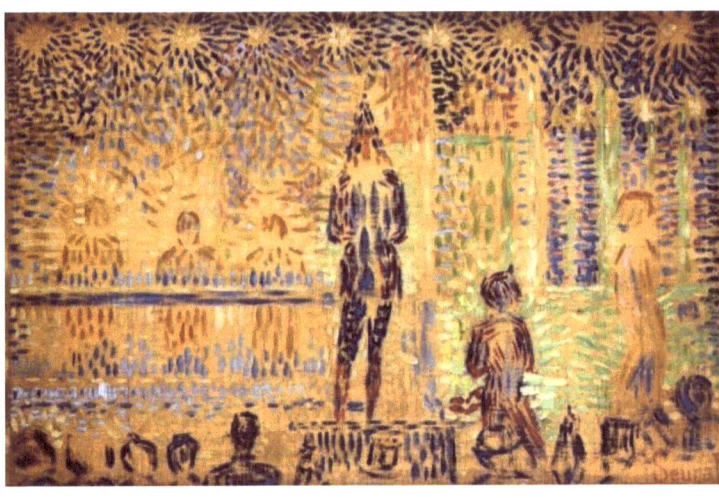

Study for 'Invitation to the Sideshow', 1888,
oil on canvas

Port-en-Bessin, The Outer Harbor, Low Tide,
1888, oil on canvas

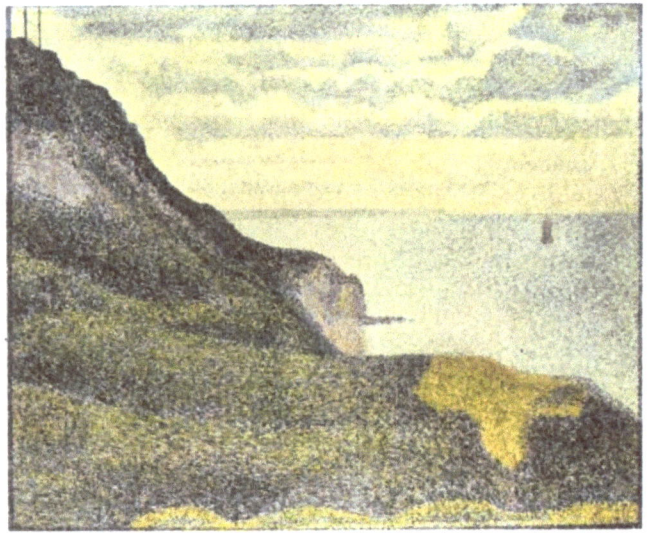

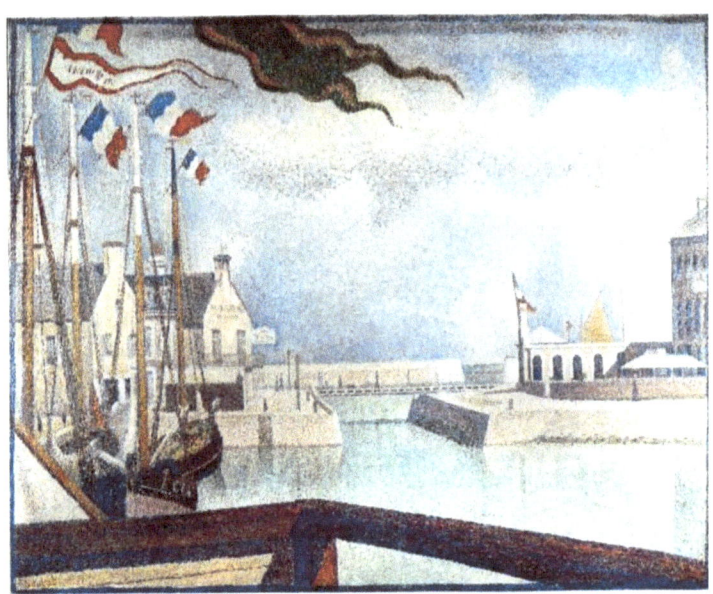

Port-en-Bessin, the Semaphore and Cliffs,
1888, oil on canvas

Sunday at Port-en-Bessin, 1888, oil on canvas

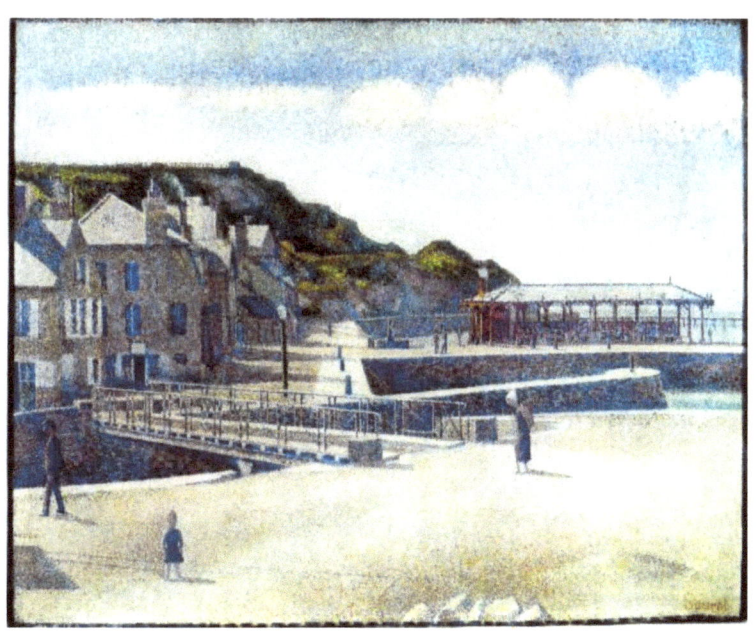

The Harbour and the Quays at Port-en-Bessin, 1888, oil on canvas

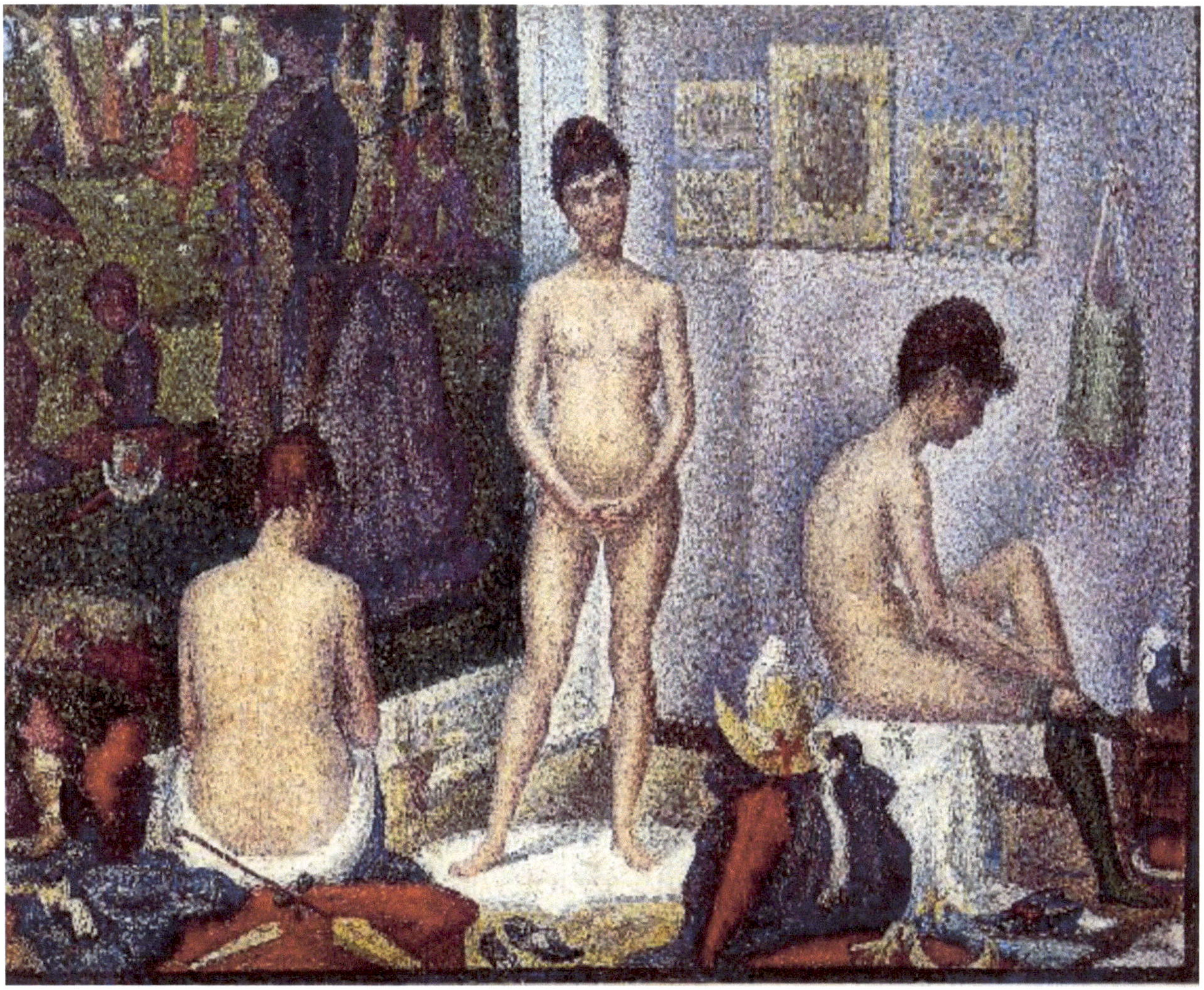

The Models, 1887-1888, oil on canvas

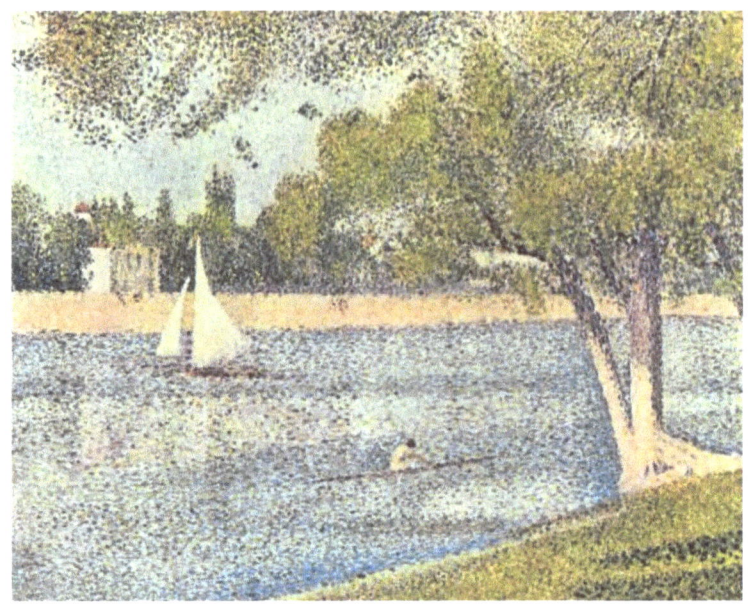

The river Seine at La Grande-Jatte, 1888, oil on canvas

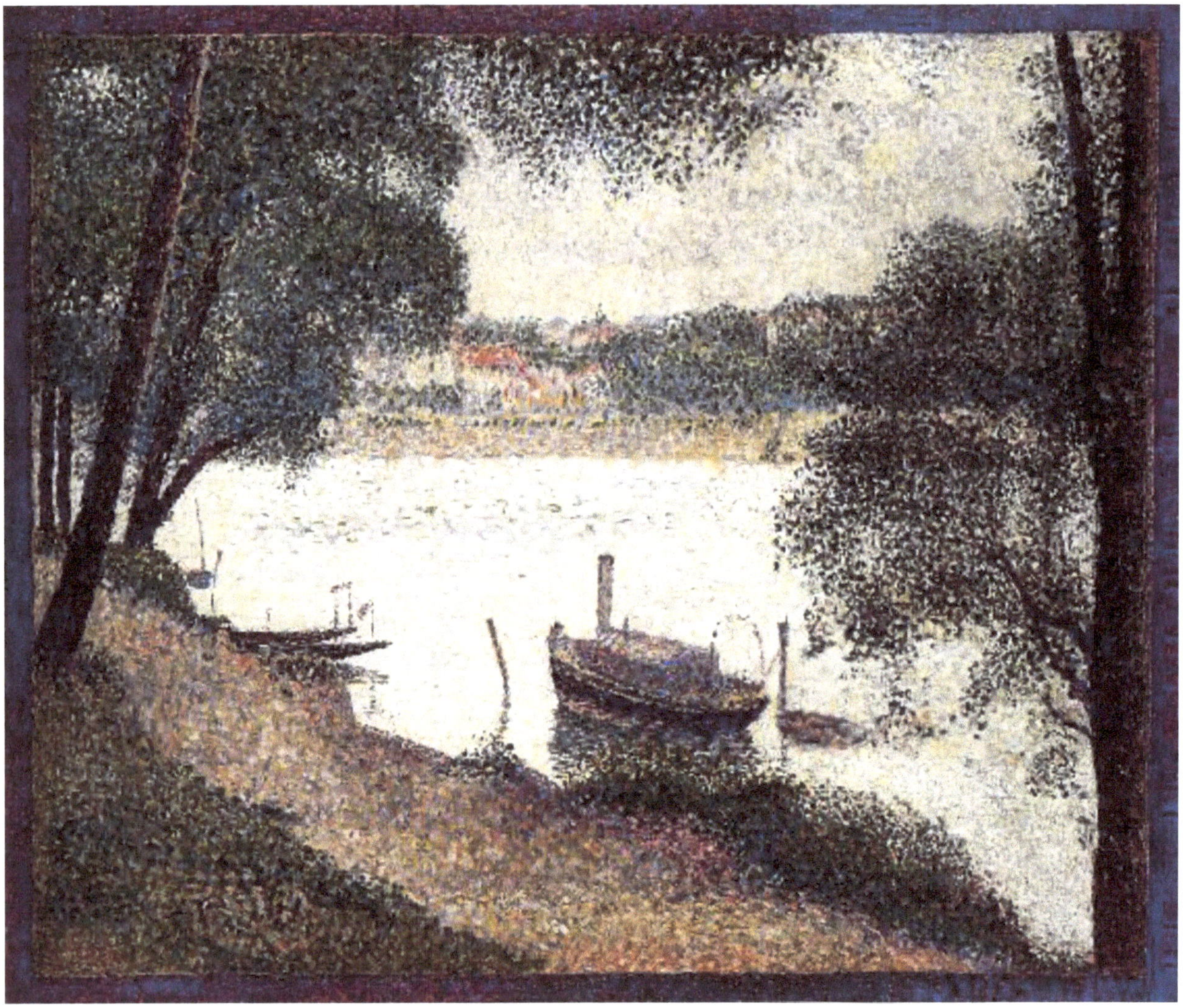

The Seine at La Grande Jatte in the Spring, 1888, oil on canvas

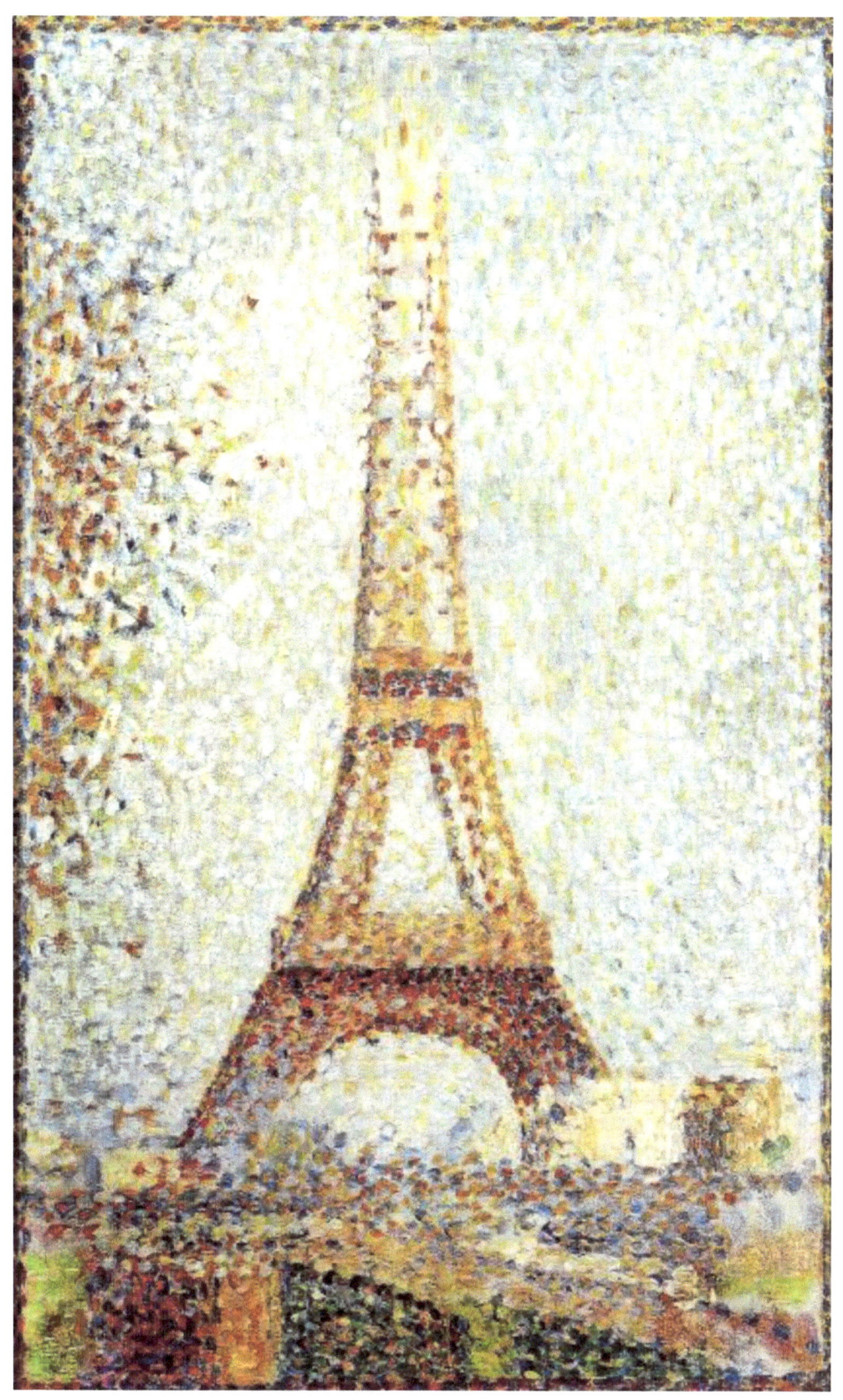

The Eiffel Tower, 1889, oil on wood

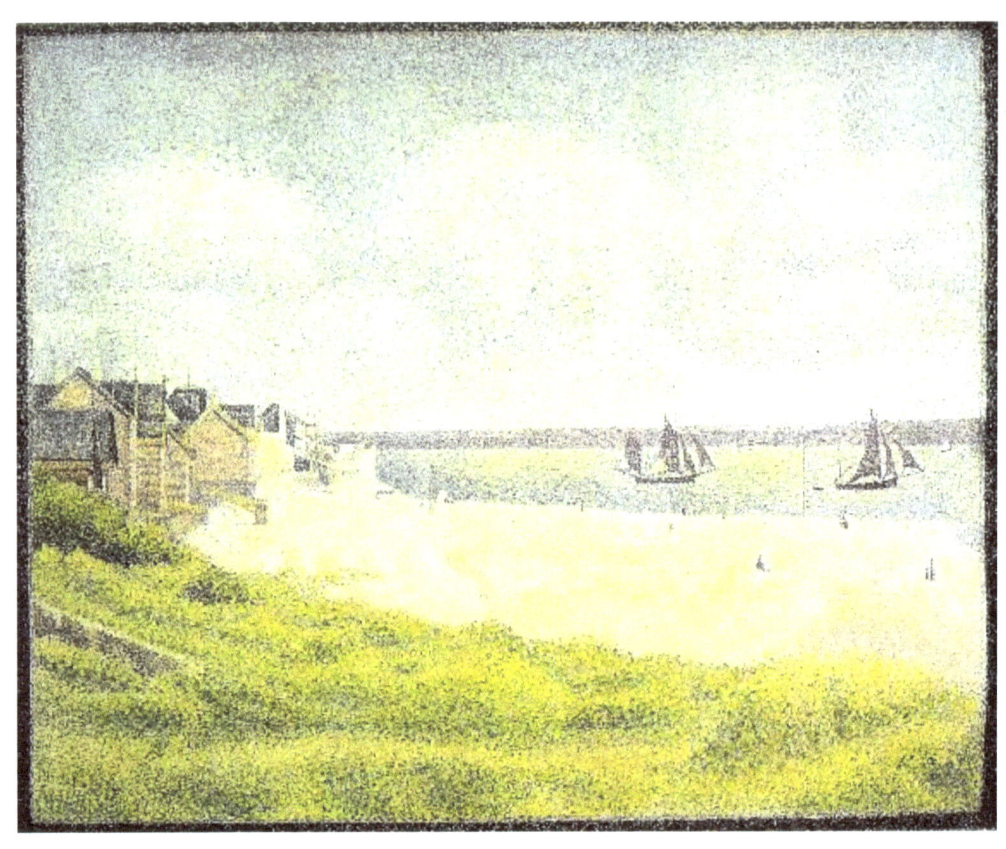

View of Crotoy, the Valley, 1889, oil on canvas

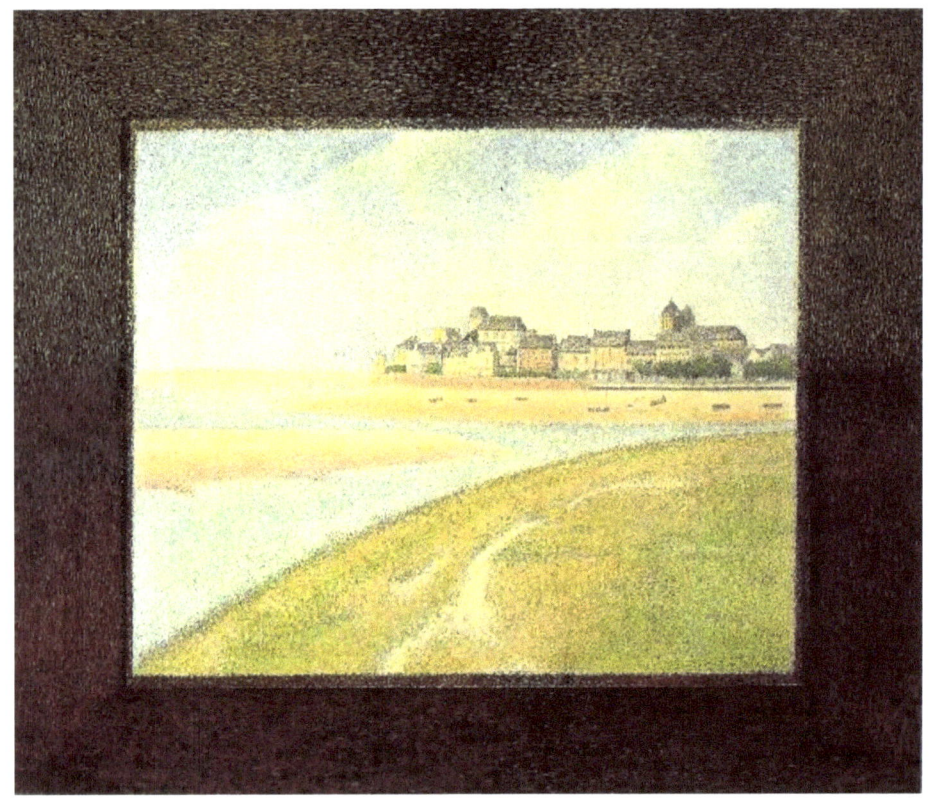

View of Le Crotoy, from Upstream, 1889, oil on canvas

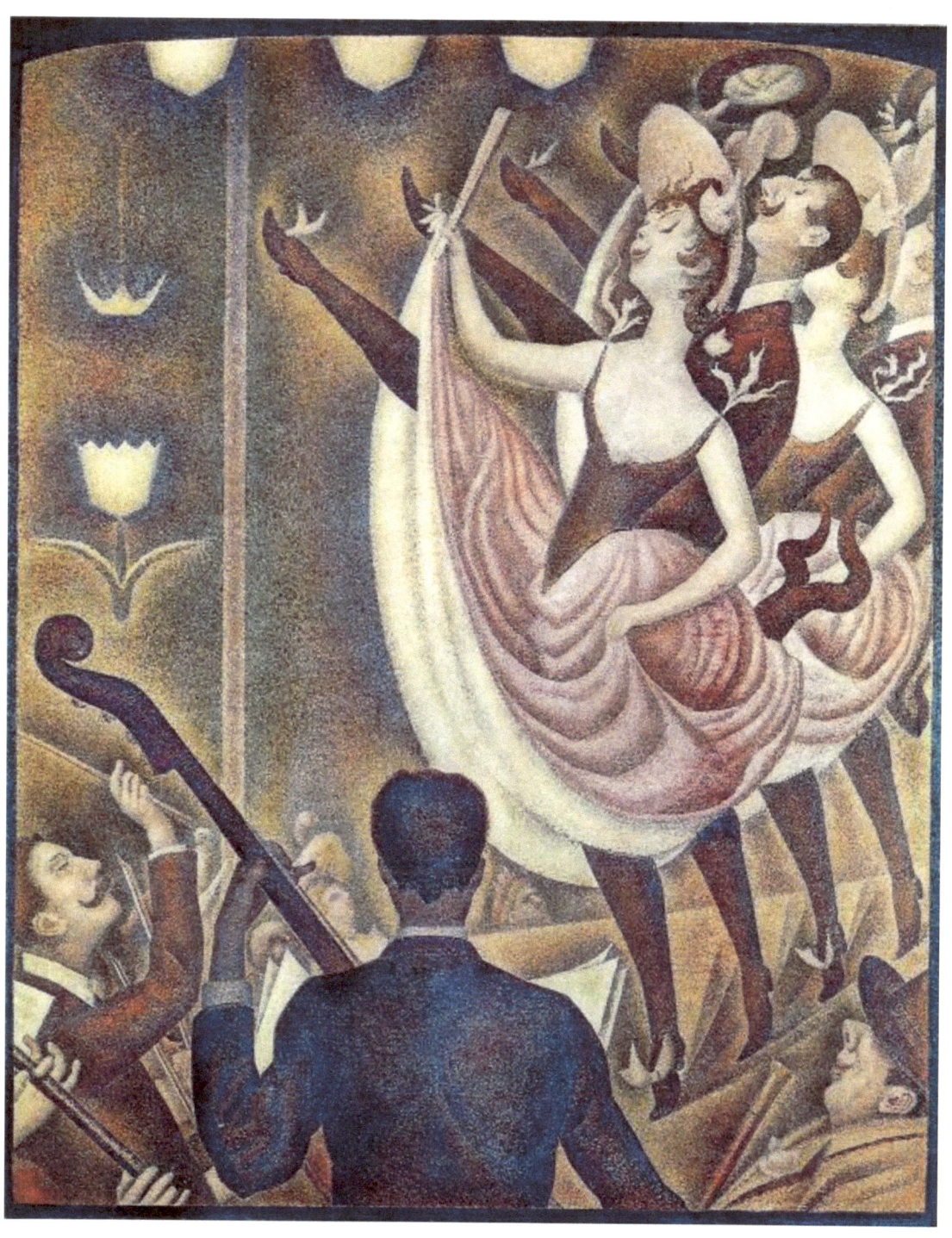

Chahut, 1889-1890, oil on canvas

In 1887-90 Seurat was working on the Circus Parade, Le Chahut and the not quite finished Circus. It was a Degas world. The effects of stage lighting, overlapping and cropped foreground figures, and a certain malice in the grotesque way types of people or posture are presented, are related to Degas. However, the differences are greater: a sense of ceremony accompanied by distortions and grimaces, motion arrested in mechanical parallel attitudes, a strict patterning of spaces, and an emphatically enigmatic flavour despite the seemingly straightforward attention-getting.

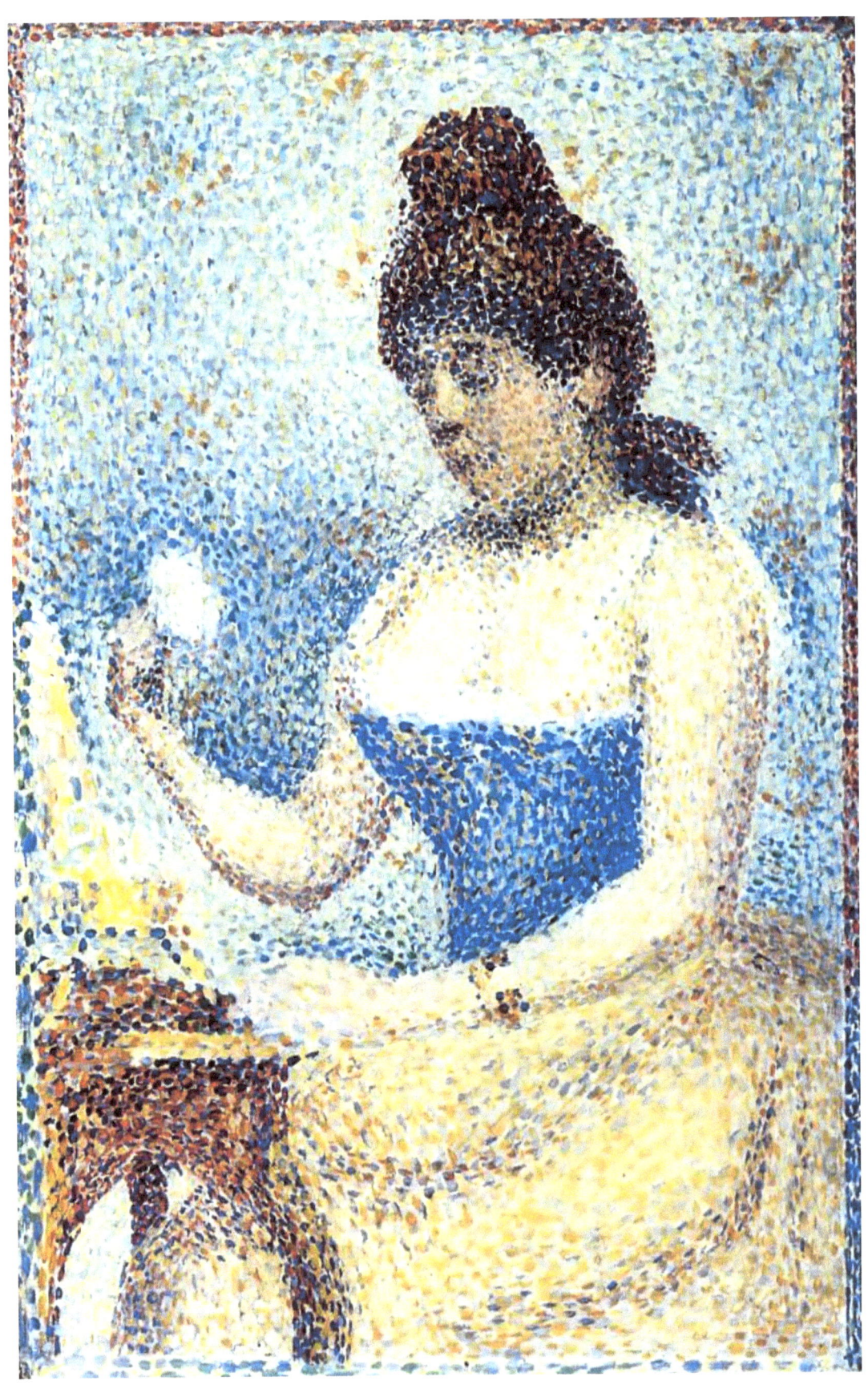

Study for "Young Woman Powdering Herself", 1889-1890, oil on wood

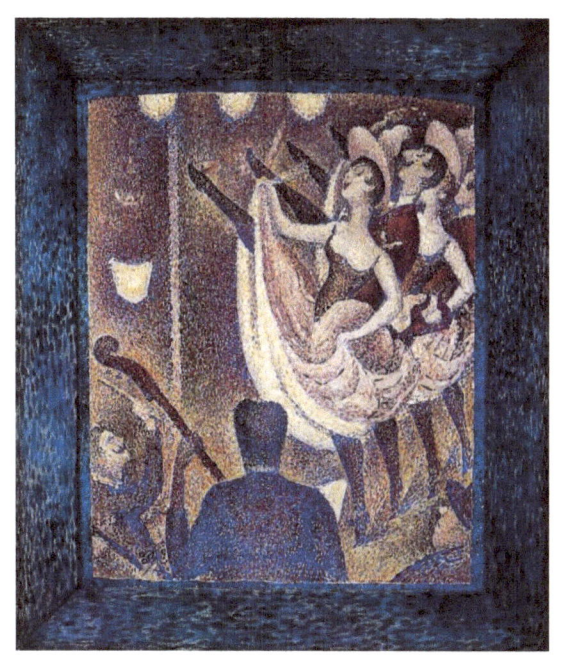

Study for 'Chahut', 1889-1890, oil

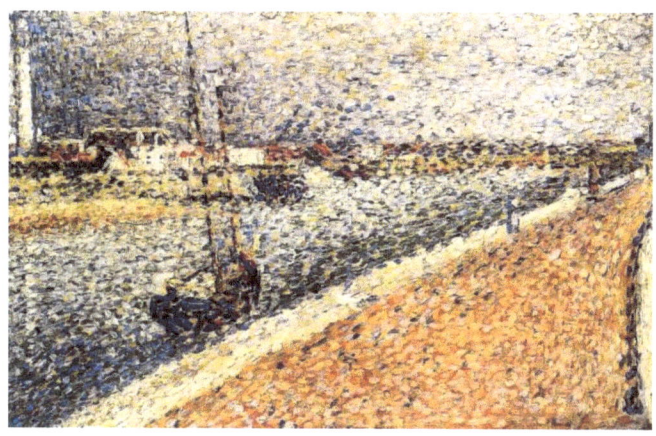

Study for 'The Channel at Gravelines', 1890, oil on canvas

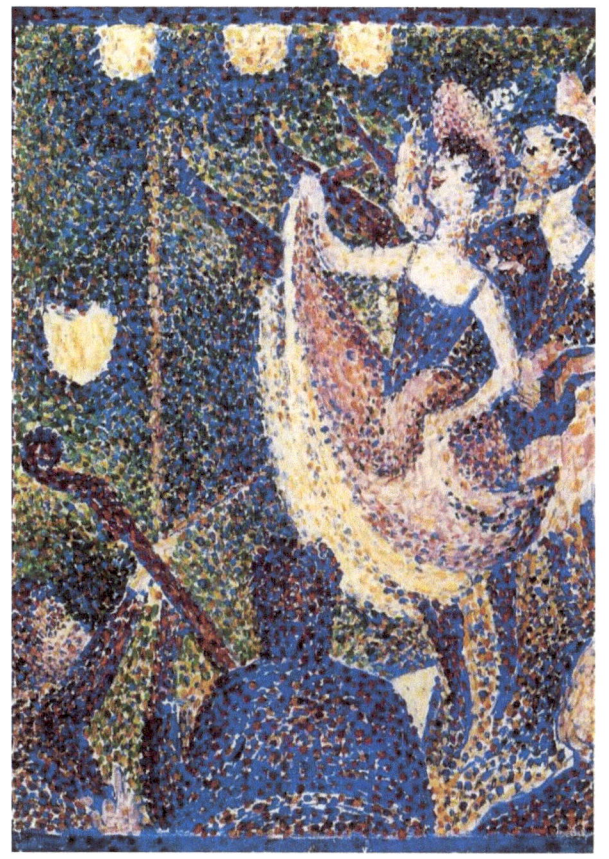

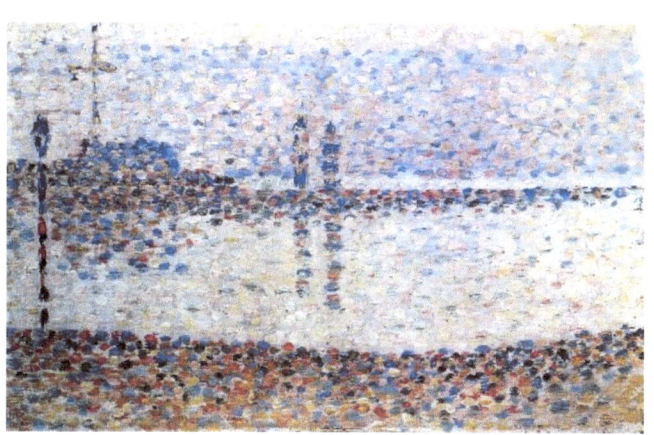

Study for 'The Channel at Gravelines, Evening', 1890, oil on wood

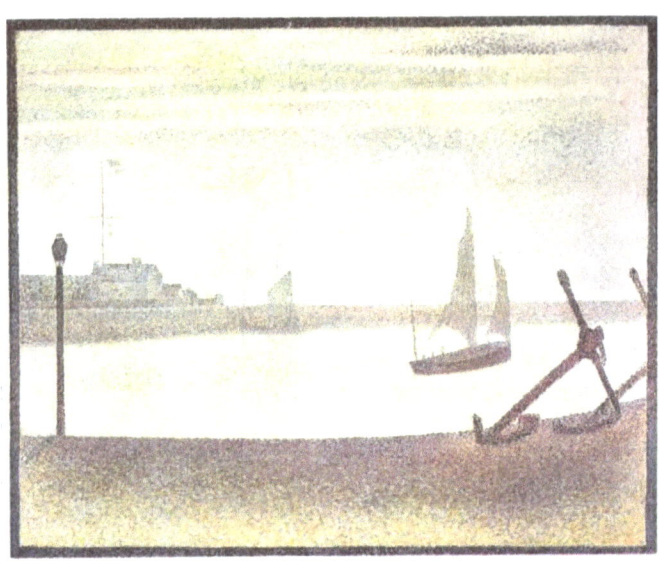

The Channel at Gravelines, Evening, 1890,
oil on canvas

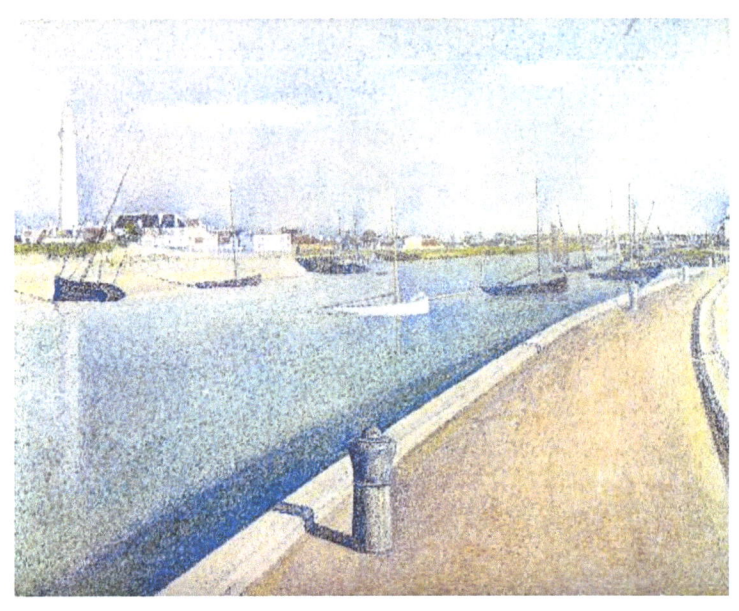

The Channel of Gravelines, Petit Fort
Philippe, 1890, oil on canvas

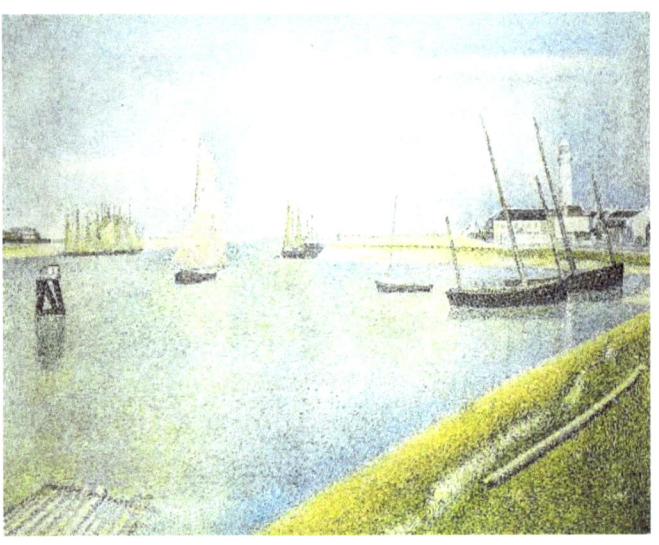

The Channel at Gravelines, in the Direction
of the Sea, 1890, oil on canvas

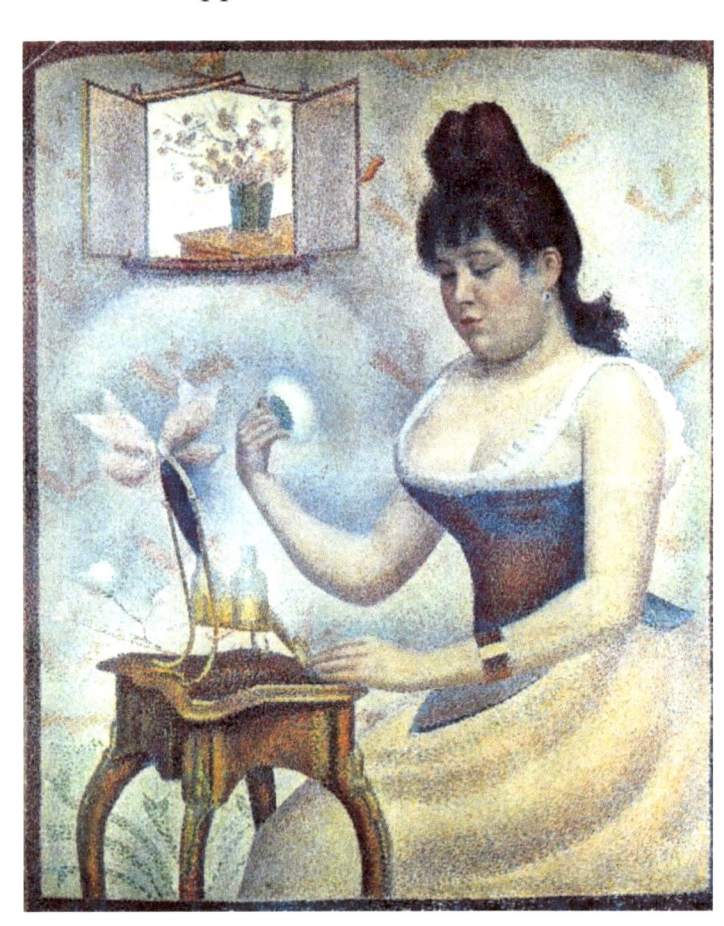

Young Woman Powdering Herself
1889-1890, oil on canvas

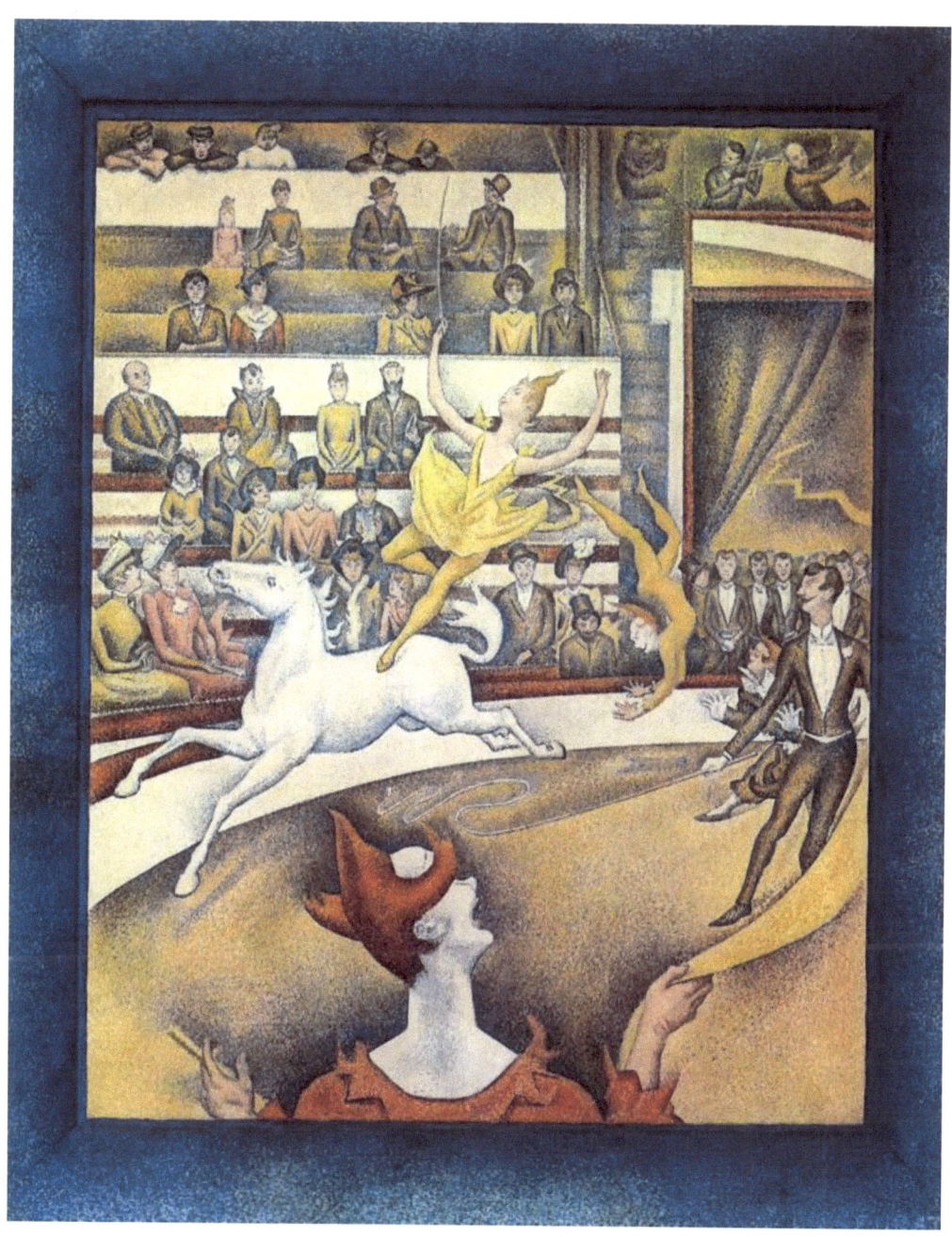

The Circus, 1890-1891, oil on canvas

Although this painting was still not completed at the painter's early death in 1891, Seurat had already exhibited it that year in the Salon des Indйpendents. It was intended to bring home clearly the principles of his art that he had developed in the previous ten years and at the same time to emphasize his leading role in modern painting.

The circus was that of the Cirque Fernando, not far from Seurat's studio. To clarify his depiction Seurat left most of the seats empty behind the artiste riding into the arena. The work has something of the quality of a poster.

The Cirque Fernando had its pitch on the Boulevard Rochechouart. In 1894 it was redesigned as a theatre. Included among its regular guests were Lautrec, and also Degas, Renoir and Seurat, who decorated the rooms with their painting.

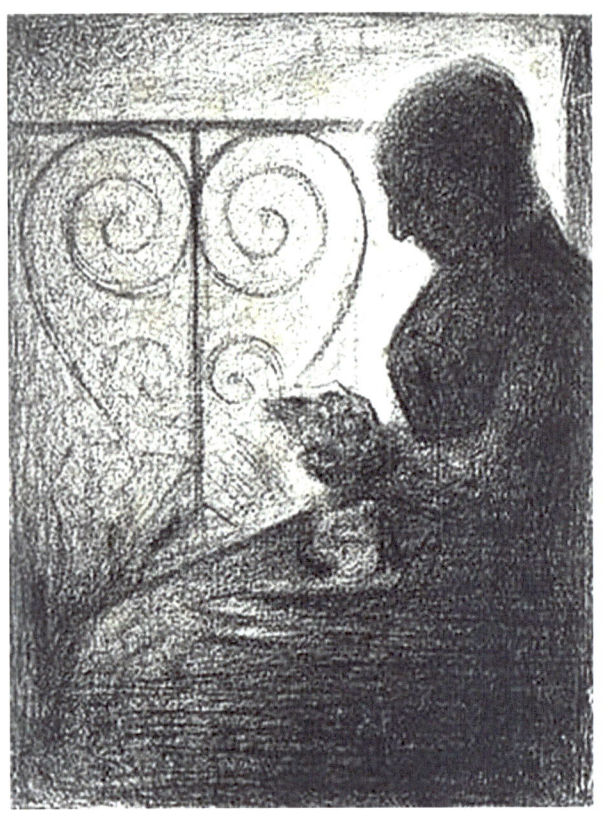

On the balcony, crayon

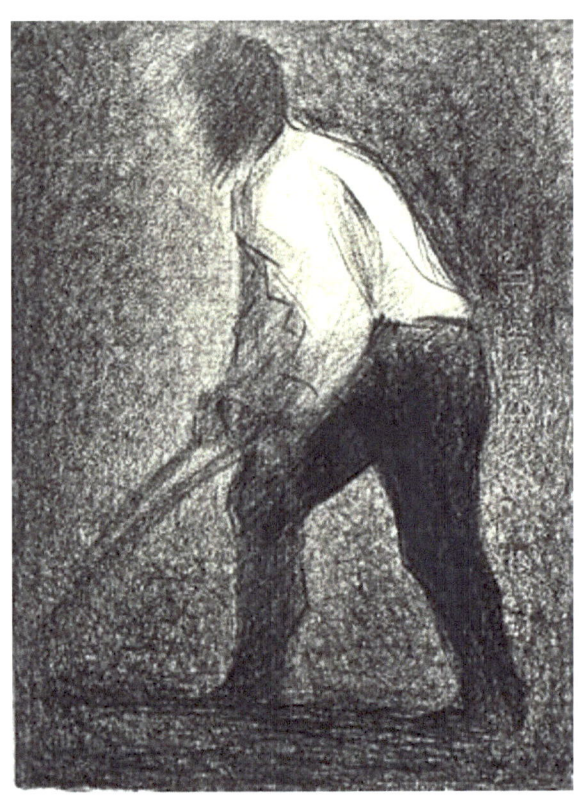

The Ploughman, crayon

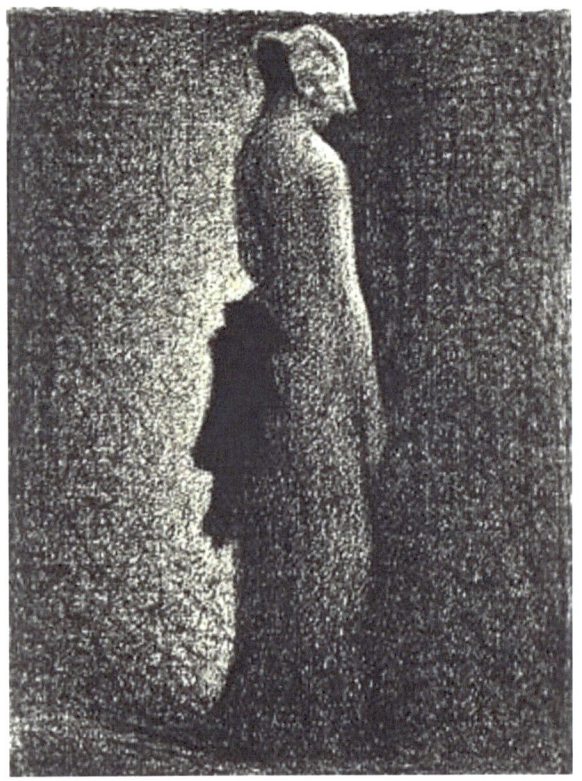

The black bow, crayon

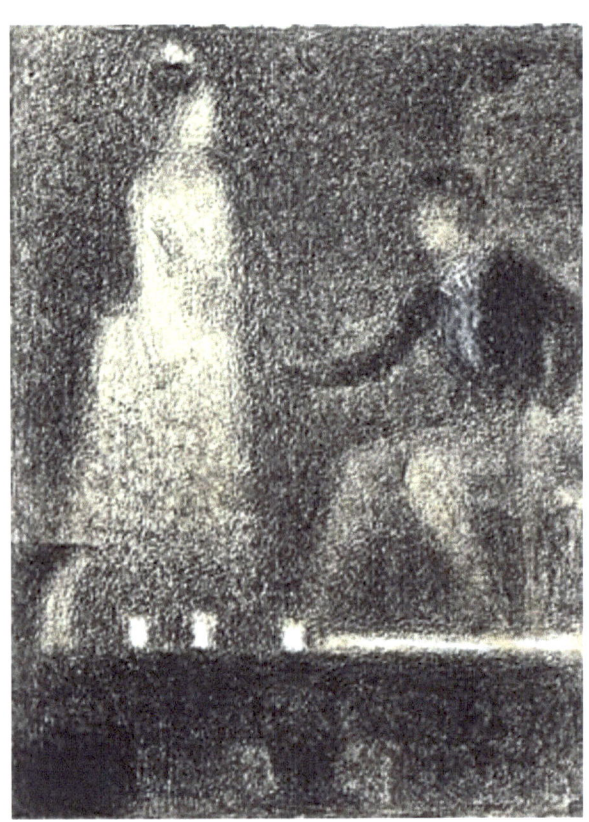

The scene in the theater, crayon

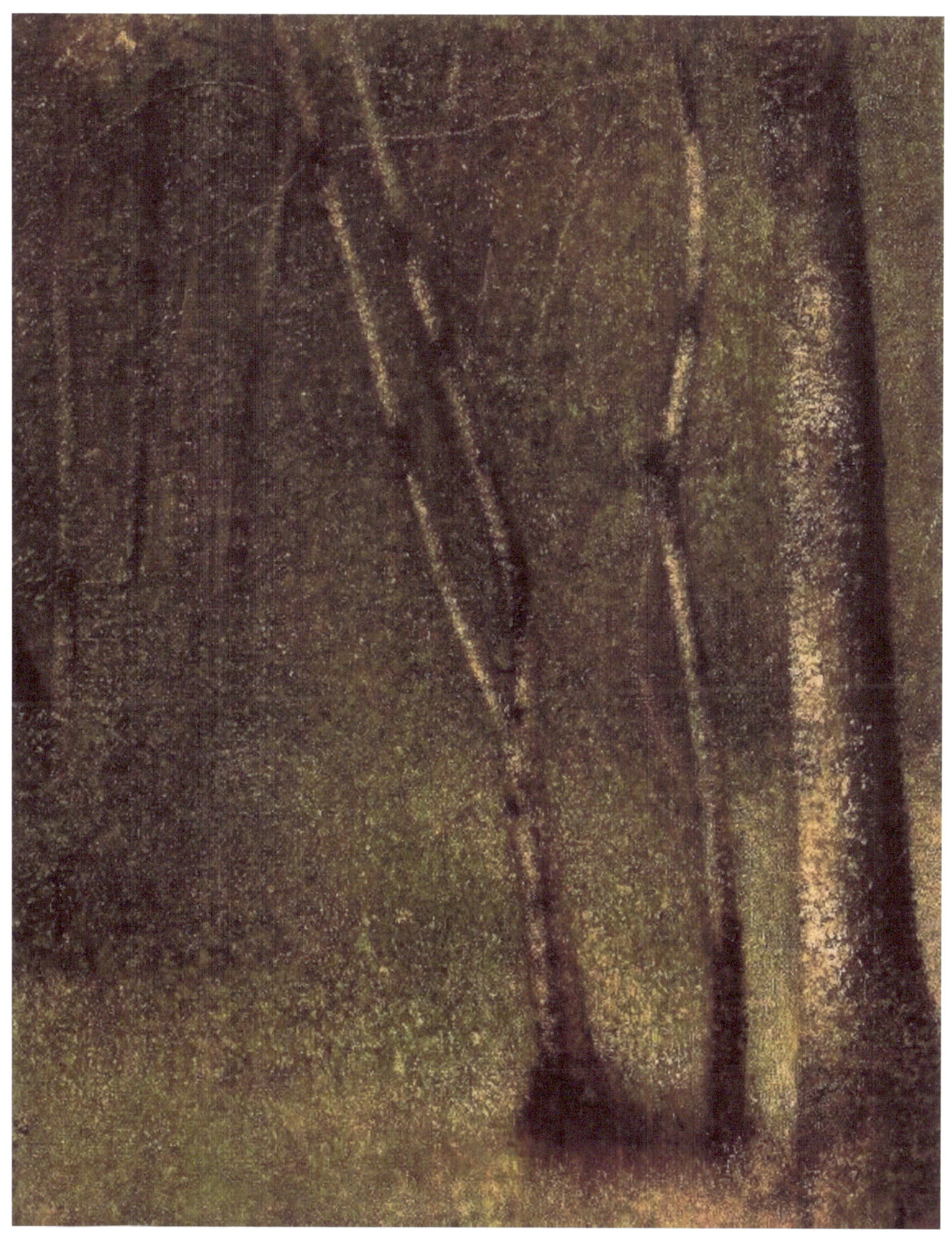

The Forest at Pontaubert, oil on canvas